MA KILEY

The Life
of a
Railroad
Telegrapher

THOMAS C. JEPSEN

SOUTHWESTERN STUDIES NO. 104

© 1997
Texas Western Press
The University of Texas at El Paso
El Paso, Texas 79968-0633

First Edition
Library of Congress Catalog No. 96-061731
ISBN 0-87404-275-5

∞

Texas Western Press books are printed on acid-free paper, meeting the guidelines for permanence and durability of the Committee on Production Guidelines for Book Longevity of the Council on Library Resources.

CONTENTS

ACKNOWLEDGMENTS

I would like to thank the following people, whose collective efforts have made it possible to bring Ma Kiley's fascinating story to life again: Marjean Friesen Binns, Ma Kiley's granddaughter, for providing a wealth of personal reminiscences, as well as her sharp-eyed editorial skills; Bennie Lou Franks Weaver, Ma Kiley's niece, for her assistance with family history and sharing family photographs; Hal Carstens of Carstens Publications, publishers of Railfan/Railroad Magazine, for permission to reprint "The Bug and I" in its original form; Jim Metlicka, Office of Public Affairs, Railroad Retirement Board, for locating Mattie Kuh's retirement records; Shirley Burman, railroad photographer and curator of "Women and the American Railroad," for helping out with railroad terminology; Howard Hooper, director, Oakland Cemetery, Dallas, Texas, for help in locating Alva Gedney Crew's grave; my wife, Marsha, for her support during the many months it took to type and assemble the manuscript; my sister Mary and her husband, Larry Wallace, for their help in navigating Dallas and locating the Oakland Cemetery; and Mary Anne Maier, for her careful editing of the final manuscript.

Ma Kiley and Her "Bug"

I stumbled across the Ma Kiley story, quite literally, in the Wentworth and Leggett Bookshop in Durham, North Carolina. I was looking for books on the railroads; something on a bookshelf caught my eye, and as I walked toward it, my foot bumped a pile of magazines on the floor. It was a stack of old copies of *Railroad Magazine* from the 1950s. *Railroad Magazine*, in its several incarnations as *Railroad, Railroad Stories, Railroad Man's Magazine,* and, most recently, as Harold Carsten's *Railfan/Railroad Magazine*, has been primarily a men's magazine that could be found in barber shops and hobby shops, as well as in the station agent's office at the railroad depot, especially during the first half of this century.

I picked up the stack of magazines and started to look through the tables of contents, hoping to find something on telegraphy. I knew retired telegraphers would sometimes write up their reminiscences and send them in, in hopes of getting them published. I had no expectation of finding anything by women operators; autobiographical writings by women telegraphers are not common, since few operators had time to keep diaries or journals. Indeed, most of what I had been able to find by women telegraphers up to that time consisted of letters written to the editors of the various nineteenth-century telegraph journals, crisply phrased and surprisingly feminist in tone for the 1860s, and terse descriptions of working careers spent at the key by the Mormon operators of the Deseret Telegraph in Utah, written as part of family histories.

I opened the cover of the July 1950 issue of *Railroad Magazine* and was surprised to find an article titled "The Bug and I" authored by one "Ma Kiley." Knowing that *bug* was telegrapher's slang for an automatic, or *Vibroplex*, telegraph key, I turned to the article, curious to see what I would find.

I wasn't disappointed. Under an illustration of the author herself ejecting an unruly male customer from her telegraph office was this summary: "For forty years I made my way in a man's world, without asking for special favors or expecting anyone to do the dirty work for me."[1]

As I read the article, the series of monochromatic stills that had previously constituted my image of the working life of women telegraph operators was transformed into a multicolored moving picture. Ma Kiley's story was an honestly written, sometimes moving account; in it, Kiley described not only her working life and her involvement with the telegraph companies and the unions, but also her personal struggles to raise children while moving constantly in search of work. It was the story of a self-reliant woman, proud of the technical skills she had acquired through her own initiative, and of her ability to make it alone. Although she would not have used the expression herself, she certainly would qualify as a feminist today.

Ma Kiley's story is surprisingly modern; like many women today in engineering and technology, she belonged to a minority of women with technical skills who chose to make a living in a highly technical, male-dominated field. Discrimination came with the territory; she constantly had to battle both overt and more subtle forms of bias. And like modern women in technical fields, she was a minority within a minority; she shared with her fellow telegraphers an arcane language that was incomprehensible to the general public, a language of train orders and telegraphic slang. As she herself noted, "It's so hard to find someone who speaks my language."[2]

Who was Ma Kiley? She was born Mattie Collins Brite in Atascosa County, Texas, near Pleasanton, in 1880, the fourth child in a family of Scotch-Irish ancestry. Her parents divorced when Mattie was seven; after remaining for a short time with her unemployed and ne'er-do-well father, Charles Henry Brite, in Atascosa County, she went to live with her mother, Alva, who had remarried to rancher Daniel G. Franks. The combined Brite and Franks families lived in Dryden, and later Eagle Pass and Del Rio, Texas.[3]

While living in Eagle Pass in 1896, Mattie met the first of her many husbands, Paul Friesen, a German who worked for the Mexican National Railroad. Out of this marriage came her first child, Carl; the marriage ended after three years due to Paul Friesen's failure to support his family. Mattie went back home to Del Rio, where her mother and stepfather managed a hotel, determined to learn a trade to support herself and her child. One of the boarders at the hotel was a telegrapher named Henry Hall; he taught Mattie the fundamentals of telegraphy and encouraged her to find work as a telegrapher.

She obtained her first railroad telegraphy position at Sabinas, Mexico, in 1902, and moved there with her son, Carl. She spent three years in northern Mexico, working in Ciudad Porfirio Díaz (now Piedras Negras), Torreón, and Durango. While in Durango in 1903, she became a member of the Order of Railroad Telegraphers (ORT), the railroad telegraphers' labor organization.

While working in Mexico, she met telegrapher Alexander John Crew "over the wire" and married him in 1904. This marriage lasted only six months; when Crew came home one night drunk and began shooting at her, Mattie left him and went back to Del Rio, where her second son, Alva Gedney Crew, was born.

For the next few years, she moved from city to city in Texas, stopping wherever she could find work as an operator. While working in Dallas, she was asked by Western Union to go to Amarillo on a short-term assignment to do some bookkeeping. Rather than take her children along, she left them at the Episcopal Children's Home in Dallas for about a week. When she returned, she found her younger child, Alva Gedney, then only two, seriously ill with a fever. He died three days later. Grief-stricken, she returned home to Del Rio and did not work for several months.

Mattie went back to work as a railroad telegrapher in Childress, Texas, in late 1907. From Childress, the railroad sent her to Wichita Falls, Texas; after a falling-out with the station agent there, she went to work for the Chicago, Rock Island, and Pacific Railroad in Waurika, Oklahoma, where she lived with Carl in a converted boxcar near the station. When she refused to send a telegram during the 1907 telegraphers' strike, she was called to railroad headquarters in Fort Worth and fired.

Mattie married and divorced John Kiley in 1908. However, she continued to go by the name of Kiley, and she was known for many years as Ma Kiley by her fellow railroaders. For the next eight years, she lived the life of a railroad *boomer*, moving incessantly throughout the western United States and Canada in search of work and a stable life. From Kansas to California, from Houston to Saskatchewan, she used her first-class skills as a telegrapher to obtain work in railroad depots and telegraph offices, moving on when there was no more work or when someone offended her sense of honor.

In July of 1916, Ma Kiley went to work for the Salt Lake Division of the Southern Pacific Railroad in Sparks, Nevada. Her boomer days were finally over; with a stable job, she sent for Carl, who had been staying with her family in Del Rio, and got him a job with the railroad as a signal maintainer. She worked for the Southern Pacific in the same part of western Nevada until her retirement twenty-six years later, in 1942.

In 1922, Ma Kiley married William Cropley; she divorced him four years later. In 1931, she married Albert Kuhn, who had, by coincidence, boarded with the Franks family in Dryden, Texas, thirty-five years before. Less than two years later, Albert Kuhn died after suffering a heart attack in Colfax, California, where he was unloading a trainload of mail.

In 1942, after being hit on the head by an order hoop carelessly thrown by a train fireman, Mattie Kuhn retired on a disability. To qualify for retirement benefits, she had to provide documentation of her work record to the Railroad Retirement Board. Her claim file is a rich and fascinating source of information on her life and work.

Railroad Magazine serialized her life story under the title "The Bug and I" in four issues in 1950, beginning with the April issue. It was widely read; in the "Reader's Choice" department of the June issue, readers voted the April installment of "The Bug and I" as the sixth most popular article in the magazine (out of a possible fifteen). Mattie Kuhn herself wrote to *Railroad Magazine* to tell the editors how proud it had made her to see her first and only writing attempt in print; her letters to the editor appeared in the "On The Spot" department in the June and July issues.

Mattie "Ma Kiley" Kuhn spent her retirement years in Napa and Atascadero, California, and Reno, Nevada. She died on 30 July 1971 at the age of 91, in Reno. Her son, Carl, a prominent Reno banker, died in 1987 at the age of 89.

"It's So Hard to Find Someone Who Speaks My Language."

Ma Kiley's language was the twice-obscure language of railroad telegraphers; it is not surprising that by 1950, she was beginning to have trouble finding people who understood her. It was a language born of the one-hundred-year union of two technologies that at first had developed in isolation from one another.

The advent of the steam-powered railroad in America dated from 1829–30, when railroads in Honesdale, Pennsylvania; Baltimore, Maryland; and Charleston, South Carolina, employed steam engines to transport goods and passengers. Samuel Morse's telegraph was first put into service in 1844 between Baltimore and Washington; its first use was to report on legislation and government business. Although early telegraph lines often followed the rail right-of-way, no attempt was made in the early years to use the telegraph as a signaling system for the railroad.

In retrospect, it seems odd that no one recognized the potential synergy of the two technologies right away. The primary problem that the early railroads faced was that of routing and scheduling on single-track systems. To prevent collisions, only one train could run on the line at a time; if a train approached from the other end of the line, one of the trains had to pull into a siding to allow the other to pass. The train that pulled into the siding was called the *inferior* train; the train that had the right-of-way was called the *superior* train.

The problem of regulating train movements was compounded by the lack of standard time zones before 1883. Each town on a rail line kept time by the sun; thus local time in New York City was six minutes ahead of the time in Philadelphia. If trains left both cities at noon and headed toward each other, a computation of when and where they would meet could be disastrously in error if the difference in sun time was not taken into account.

The railroads devised numerous stratagems to circumvent these problems. The earliest railroads sent a flagman ahead of the train on foot to watch for approaching trains; this had the disadvantage of reducing the maximum speed to that of a man's walk. A more expensive approach was to install double tracks, one for each direction. This increased speed but the cost made it impractical.[4]

The first person to see the possibilities of using the telegraph for signaling was Charles Minot, superintendent of the Erie Railroad in 1851. He proposed to the directors of the railroad that a telegraph line be built alongside the railroad tracks to be used in conducting railroad business. The directors scoffed at his then-radical suggestion, arguing that it would be too expensive to operate; Minot countered that the telegraph could be run by railroad station agents and clerks in their spare time. Having obtained grudging permission to proceed, Minot had a line built between Goshen, New York, and the railroad's Piermont, New York, terminus on the Hudson River. The line was used to send messages ahead regarding railroad freight shipments; for example, a farmer who was shipping cattle from Goshen to New York City would telegraph ahead to Piermont to have a barge ready to transport the cattle down the river. Minot surmised that the telegraph might also be used for regulating the movement of trains. An engineer, while stopping at each station, could have the telegrapher ask the next town if any trains had passed the station, and, if the answer was no, could safely proceed down the track. Additionally, if he was operating a superior train, the engineer could ask the telegrapher to order the stationmaster at the next town to hold any trains at the station until the superior train passed.

Minot first put his idea into practice in June 1851 while traveling westward on one of his trains toward Goshen, New York. His train, the inferior train, had pulled off the track at Turners, New York, and was waiting for the superior train from the other direction to pass. After waiting several minutes for the train to appear, Minot went to the telegraph office and asked the operator to inquire of the operator in Goshen if the other train had passed the station yet. When the reply came back that the train had not yet passed, Minot had the operator send an order to the Goshen operator to hold the train at the Goshen station until his train cleared. Minot then ordered the engineer of his train, Isaac Lewis, to proceed toward Goshen. Lewis, distrustful of the new technology, refused, telling Minot, "Do you take me for a damn fool? I won't run by that thing!" Lewis then retreated to the caboose, which he felt to be the safest place in the event of a crash. Minot took charge of the train himself and drove it to Goshen, where he arrived safely without incident.[5]

It took about a decade for telegraphic routing to become commonplace. The telegraph brought about a tremendous increase in efficiency, cutting the time it took to get from place to place by as much as half. The work soon created its own language. A dispatcher, or *DS,* at a central location would plan a route and schedule for a train, and transmit it to all the telegraphers (known as *ops* or *brass pounders*) at each order station *(OS)* along the line. Each telegrapher would notify the other stations on the line when the train passed; this was called OSing the train. This knowledge would enable the next operator down the line to determine when the train would arrive. If the train needed to be held at a station, or if the routing needed to be changed, the telegraph operator would write out the orders received from the dispatcher and hand them to the conductor of the train when it stopped. Even if the train was not scheduled to stop at the station, the operator could hold out the orders on an *order hoop*, usually a bamboo pole with a hoop at the end, and a member of the crew would grab the orders from the engine window. If an inferior train needed to be moved to a siding to permit a superior train to pass, either the telegrapher or the station agent would operate the switch levers to connect the track to the siding.

The railroads began to work out a mutually advantageous strategy with the commercial telegraph companies in the 1860s and 1870s. The telegraph company would install and maintain the telegraph lines alongside the tracks and provide the instruments in each depot. The railroad, in turn, would pay the wages of an operator who would not only OS trains, but would also transmit personal messages, news reports, and commodity reports for the telegraph company. The *op* often doubled as station agent, express agent, or ticket seller—or a combination of all four. Thus the railroad got a signaling system maintained by the telegraph company, and the telegraph company got a telegraph station in many small towns and railroad crossings where an office would not otherwise be economically justifiable.

Telegraphers quickly developed a shorthand language, almost incomprehensible to outsiders, that they used over the lines. Operators identified themselves by a sign (sometimes spelled *sine*) which could be a nickname or just a two- or three-letter code; they also had a *station code*, that identified the station at which they operated. Number codes were also used; *30* signified the end of a lengthy message, while *73* meant "best wishes." A quick way to ask who was at the key at the other end was to use the code *134*.[6]

The work began to be automated in the 1890s with the advent of telephone dispatching and *block signaling*. Although the telephone gradually took over much of the commercial business of sending personal messages, it never completely replaced the telegraph for train dispatching. It did not provide any improvement in speed, since train orders could only be dictated as fast as the operator could copy them down, and provided no improvement in accuracy. As words were spoken rather than spelled out, errors were more likely, requiring telephone dispatchers to repeat each order to verify correctness.

Block signaling provided a significant improvement over simple telegraphic dispatching. Block signaling gave the dispatcher information on the location of trains within each *block*, or section of track. It also provided the engineer with a visual indication of what lay ahead. If the signal light at the beginning of a block was green, it meant that the engineer could proceed. An amber (or clear) signal indicated that it was safe to enter the block, but somewhere ahead there was another train on the track. If the signal was red, however, it meant that a train was approaching from the other direction and that a collision was possible. An engineer seeing a red signal would immediately pull into a siding to let the train from the other direction pass. Although block signaling automated some of the telegrapher's work, telegraphers were still needed to communicate order changes from the dispatcher to the crew of each train and to notify other stations of block signal changes.

Centralized Traffic Control, or CTC, first introduced in the 1920s, began to eliminate the need for railroad telegraphers. CTC made it possible not only to know the location of trains at a central location, but also to control routing from a central location and to communicate directly with train crews via radio. A computerized form of CTC is used today to route trains across the entire United States from just a few locations.[7]

However, it took a long time for the railroads to completely replace telegraphers with automated systems. Telegraphers continued to operate at remote rural stations until well into the 1970s; even at larger offices, the telegraph system was left in place as a backup in case of emergency.

Ma Kiley owed her entry into the profession of railroad telegraphy in part to the rapid expansion of the railroads in Texas and Mexico around the turn of the century. The railroad boom that swept the rest of the United States in the mid-nineteenth century did not arrive in Texas until after the Civil War. As late as 1870, Texas had only 583 miles of railroad, mostly concentrated in the eastern part of the state. During the next decade, the growth of the Texas railroad system began in earnest as the railroad companies acquired land grants and started to expand. As in other parts of the West, the railroad's role in moving crops, raw materials, and people across vast expanses quickly made it a vital element in the economic growth of post–Civil War Texas. Expansion of the railroads was so rapid that thirty-five years later, Texas would boast the highest rail mileage of any state—more than ten thousand miles in 1904.[8]

At the same time that the railroads were expanding in Texas, rapid growth was occurring in the Mexican railroad industry. Porfirio Díaz encouraged the growth of the railroads, often financed by foreign capital, during his presidencies (1877–80, 1884–1911). Since Mexico's main trading partner was the United States, most of the rail lines ran toward the U.S. border, with the main rail line, the Mexican National Railroad, running from Mexico City to El Paso and Laredo, Texas. By 1910, Mexico had 24,717 kilometers, or approximately 14,830 miles, of track. Rapid expansion of the railroads created a demand for skilled workers; many foreigners, including Americans like Ma Kiley, went to Mexico to work for the railroads during this era.[9]

"I Got Into the Game Myself."

When Ma Kiley first began to copy Morse code in the Del Rio, Texas, depot in 1901, she was by no means the first woman to work as a railroad telegrapher—a fact she was probably well aware of. Women had been working for the railroads in a variety of capacities since the late 1830s and had been working as railroad telegraphers since 1855.[10]

In fact, women were working as telegraphers before Minot integrated telegraphy into the railroad system. Sarah G. Bagley, the mill worker and women's rights activist who founded the Lowell Female Labor Reform Association, became the telegraph operator in Lowell, Massachusetts, in 1846, only two years after Morse first demonstrated his invention. Helen Mills became a telegraph operator in Greenville, Pennsylvania, in 1850. And in 1851, the same year that Minot gave the first train order, Emma Hunter became the telegraph operator in West Chester, Pennsylvania.[11]

Elizabeth Cogley, the first woman to become a railroad telegrapher of whom we have any record, started out as a messenger for the Atlantic and Ohio Telegraph Company in Lewistown, Pennsylvania, in 1852. Starting out as a messenger was a common career path for male telegraphers in the nineteenth century, but it was unusual for a woman. Like Ma Kiley, Cogley learned Morse code from a telegraph operator who boarded with the family, and she began to operate in 1855. When the office of the Atlantic and Ohio was moved into the Pennsylvania Railroad station in the winter of 1855–56, she became the Pennsylvania Railroad's first official female operator.[12]

The earliest telegraph receivers used a *register* that recorded the received signals on a paper tape for later decoding; this was referred to as *receiving by sight*. This quickly proved inefficient, particularly for the railroads, where it was necessary to quickly decode received messages. Operators soon learned to decode an incoming message immediately by listening to the clicking of the register as it marked or embossed the paper tape and writing down the message as it was received. This was called *receiving by sound* and it became standard practice in the mid-1850s. Telegraph instrument manufacturers eventually removed the paper tape assembly from their receivers, which became known as *sounders*.

The Baltimore and Ohio Railroad, wishing to train its employees in this new technique, opened a school for telegraphers in Pittsburgh, Pennsylvania, around 1860; it admitted both men and women. Two of the students at the B & O school during the Civil War era were Abbie G. Struble and her sister, Madge. Abbie turned out to be the best pupil in the class and was the first operator allowed to receive by sound on that line. After her marriage to J. L. Vaughan, Abbie Struble became a legend among railroad operators as "Mother Vaughan." She operated in Mexico for the Mexican National Railroad from 1891 to 1912 and opened a telegraphic school for women in Long Beach, California, during World War I.[13]

The Civil War brought about the first large increase in the number of women employed as telegraphers as men went off to war, leaving vacancies in telegraph offices. Many of these vacancies were filled by women who had previously served as unofficial assistants to their husbands or fathers. For women who were already experienced telegraphers, the Civil War provided a career boost. Elizabeth Cogley's skill and experience brought her to the attention of Pennsylvania Railroad officials; in 1864, she was transferred to railroad headquarters in Harrisburg, where she remained until her retirement in 1900.

After the Civil War, Western Union began to dominate the American telegraph industry. By absorbing its two largest rivals, the American Telegraph Company and the United States Telegraph Company, in 1866, Western Union became a $40-million monopoly that owned more than 100,000 miles of telegraph lines, connecting virtually every town in the United States.[14]

The giant company, which previously had been slow to hire women, developed a policy of actively encouraging the entry of women into the field of telegraphy. It saw the employment of women at lower wages than men as a way of remaining competitive, as stated in an 1869 trade journal:

> With the pressure constantly being brought to bear on telegraph companies to cheapen rates, with competing lines drawing off that portion of the business which provided the margins of

profit, and with the multiplication of short lines connecting factories and foundries with central offices, we expect to see demands made for women to serve in telegraph offices far beyond what now exists.

. . . Marriage to them [women] is home and an end of personal money-making for support. Thus they accept terms inferior to men because they need support only until the marriage state provides it.[15]

One result of Western Union's strategy was to create competition between men and women for jobs. Male telegraphers feared that they would lose their jobs to women, who would perform the same work for less money; they countered by accusing their female co-workers of making more errors and being prone to nervous conditions.[16]

However, it was not the employment of women but a slow-moving economy that caused telegraphers' wages to fall in the late 1860s and early 1870s. In an attempt to maintain Civil War–era wages, the commercial operators banded together to form a union and struck against Western Union on 3 January 1870. The strike was shortlived; Western Union called in strikebreakers, and on 18 January the labor action was called off. Western Union refused to hire many of the strikers back. Women operators felt that the giant company was being particularly vindictive toward them.[17]

Some of the women strikers, unable to find work as commercial operators, became railroad operators, a pattern that would become common in later strikes. Others went west in search of employment. "F," an operator for the Laramie Division of the Union Pacific Railroad, wrote to the *Telegrapher* in February 1870 to encourage women operators to go west and work for the railroads. He mentioned that one woman was already employed on his line.[18]

Male telegraphers had already developed a reputation for a footloose lifestyle and a willingness to relocate in search of a better job. Those who moved frequently from job to job were referred to as *boomers*, to differentiate them from the *home guard*, who stayed put in one place. During the economic turmoil of the 1870s, female boomers began to appear as well. Mostly young and single, they took advantage of the free passes offered to telegraphers by many of the railroads to relocate in search of better jobs.

One such boomer was Fannie Wheeler, daughter of the station agent in Vinton, Iowa, in the late 1860s. Her upwardly mobile career took her first to Waterloo, Iowa, and then to the Chicago Western Union office, where she managed the newly created Ladies' Department in 1869. She then headed west, first to Omaha and then San Francisco, where she operated in 1875. Later she moved down the California coast to Los Angeles, and then, in 1876, to Santa Barbara. Her hometown paper, the *Vinton Eagle,* kept readers apprised of her whereabouts and boasted of her success in a male-dominated field: "Who shall say *such accomplishments* are unladylike and unrefined."[19]

The number of women employed in telegraph offices continued to increase in the last quarter of the nineteenth century. By 1897, the sight of "a young woman presiding over the telegraph in offices and railway stations" was, according to reformer Frances Willard, so ordinary an occurrence "that one has ceased to have even a feeling of surprise at seeing them there."[20] Although Ma Kiley was probably the only woman learning Morse code in the Del Rio depot in 1901, her career soon brought her into contact with many other women who made their living at the key at the beginning of the twentieth century.

"She Thinks She Will Learn to Telegraph."

Ma Kiley spent most of her career at the key in railroad depot telegraph offices, where an operator was typically a jack-of-all-trades; there were trains to be OSed, orders from the DS to be copied and hooped up to passing trains, freight to be tariffed and tracked, tickets to be sold, and train lists to be compiled. The depot telegraph office was generally located in the telegrapher's window, a sort of bay window that protruded from the side of the depot building toward the railroad tracks. The telegrapher's window was frequently glassed in on all three sides to give the telegrapher a clear view of all arriving and departing trains.

In small stations, the person in charge was the station agent; he, or occasionally she, had to sell tickets, keep the station books, switch the tracks, set the signals, and telegraph. In addition, the station agent had to deal with the public. In the words of B. B. Adams, editor of the *Railroad Gazette,* the agent had to be "ready, like the conductor to submit to some abuse from ill-bred customers." Sometimes a woman would take over a station agency formerly run by her husband. When G. W. Hill died in 1884, his wife, Cassie, took over the Roseville, California, depot and moved in with their five children, serving as station agent, Wells Fargo agent, and telegraph operator while raising her children on the job.[21]

Ma Kiley was technically the station agent at Dodge, North Dakota, in 1908, although, as she commented, "there never was any agency work performed there and the mice chewed up the tickets." Most of her working life was spent in medium-sized stations where the work was divided among two to ten employees. In addition to the stationmaster, who managed the station, there was usually a ticket agent, a freight agent, a baggage master, and a telegrapher. Of these, only the telegrapher was likely to be a woman; as B. B. Adams observed, at railroad stations "where the business has increased enough to warrant the employment of an assistant, a young woman to do the telegraphing is frequently the first helper engaged."[22]

The depot personnel had to work in close contact with the train crews. Train crews consisted of an engineer, a conductor, one or more firemen, and several brakemen. The engineer drove the train and regulated the speed and boiler pressure, while the firemen stoked the fire and shoveled coal. The brakemen were responsible for operating the hand brakes used on nineteenth-century trains and also for coupling and decoupling cars. The conductor took tickets on passenger trains, and was responsible for seeing to it that the train left each station on schedule. Section masters were responsible for a crew of three to ten men who maintained the tracks around a station. Typically a single section crew was responsible for maintenance of three to ten miles of track.[23]

The person with whom a telegrapher spent most of his or her time communicating over the wires was the dispatcher, or DS, who controlled the movement of all the trains in his or her district and had to know where each train was at all times. The dispatcher originated all train orders and telegraphed them to individual order stations (OSs). Women dispatchers were rare but did exist; one was Rebecca S. Bracken, who was chief operator and dispatcher for the Michigan Central Railroad in Niles, Michigan, for nearly forty years before retiring in 1905.[24]

Railroad operators had to master specialized railroad equipment as well as the telegraphic instruments. Operators might have to manually change signaling flags and track routing by means of interlocking the switch levers, a formidable task in the days of the nonautomatic "Armstrong" levers that required considerable exertion to operate. They had to learn to use order hoops for handing orders to passing trains, and signaling flags and a red lantern for signaling and flagging trains. There were tariffs and waybills to be completed for freight shipments, and specialized forms for train routing.

Ma Kiley also spent a considerable amount of time working as a commercial operator. This involved not only sending and receiving personal messages, but also copying press and commodities reports. In larger towns that had outgrown the depot telegraph office, the commercial telegraph office was often in the downtown business district, near banks and stores. Ma Kiley's first commercial job was in such an office in Del Rio in 1905. Hotels sometimes maintained offices to handle dispatches for their visitors. General stores also occasionally housed an operator's table.

A well-defined hierarchy of jobs existed in the commercial telegraph office. The manager oversaw the general operations of the office. This included the hiring and firing of personnel, assignments and promotions, handling payroll and recordkeeping, as well as serving as a liaison to corporate headquarters. Typically the manager was a telegrapher who had come up through the ranks, as operator and then chief operator. Although the majority of managers were men, it was not uncommon for a woman to manage a telegraph office; Ma Kiley was the manager of the Del Rio, Texas, Western Union office in 1905, although the job paid only fifty dollars a month.

Operators were responsible for transmitting and receiving messages in Morse code. Like Ma Kiley, most learned to operate through a combination of self-study and apprenticeship. The first run on the operator hierarchy was an entry-level or *second-class* operator. Typically this was an operator who could receive and transmit at ten or twenty words per minute with relatively few errors. He or she would be assigned the less demanding and slower work such as personal messages and local traffic. For Ma Kiley, being a second-class operator in 1902 meant low-paying work in Mexico, mostly at nights; there was always the possibility of being bumped by an operator with more seniority, as happened to her in Durango, Mexico, in 1903.

After she acquired enough seniority and skill, Ma Kiley became a *first-class* operator, a title she used with great pride. To qualify as a first-class operator, one had to be able to send and receive error-free code at thirty to forty words per minute. Typically, five years of experience were required to become a first-class operator. First-class operators were assigned the more critical business traffic and press reports. Although this work paid better, it was often boring and tedious, as it consisted of little more than nonstop sending and receiving at high speed.

As Ma Kiley discovered when she first went to work for Western Union in 1905, sending a commercial telegram was far more complex and formal than receiving a train order in a railroad depot. There were many different classes of messages. A *day letter* was the standard-priority daytime telegram; a *full-rate* message was a higher-priority rush message. (In telegraphic terminology, a *letter* had a fixed length, say fifty words, and a flat-rate charge, while a *message* was of unspecified length and was charged by the word.) A full-rate message had priority over everything (except government messages, which had the highest priority of all). *Night letters* and *night messages* were less expensive; they were sent at night, when the line was less busy. However, there was also less chance that the operator at the receiving end would be awake and at the key. A night letter might not be delivered before the next day, and a night message would definitely not be delivered before the next day.[25]

The primary requirement for the job, of course, was expert knowledge of Morse code. All American telegraphers used the standard version of Morse code; operators at the stations that terminated the Atlantic submarine cable had to also know international Morse, which used slightly different symbols for certain letters.

It was important to have a smooth, graceful sending style; beginners were often accused of sending in an awkward, choppy style. *Clipping* was an affected sending mannerism in which the proper duration was not given to each dot or dash; male telegraphers frequently accused women of clipping. Sending styles were so personalized that most telegraphers on a given line could recognize who was sending by style alone. There are numerous stories, particularly from the Civil War era, of telegraphers masquerading as someone else but being given away by their sending styles.

Telegraph operators were often victims of an occupational hazard they called *glass arm* or *telegrapher's cramp*, now known as repetitive motion syndrome or carpal tunnel syndrome, due to the nature of the hand operation used to send Morse code continually at high speed. Ma Kiley's only reported bout with this affliction occurred in 1907–08, when, after a full day of sending press reports from a Prohibitionist convention, she recalled that "my whole left side felt paralyzed."[26] Martha Rayne described the condition in her 1893 book on work for women, *What Can A Woman Do?*:

There is the disease known as telegraph cramp, the diagnosis of
which has not yet been thoroughly ascertained by the physicians.
An operator stretches out her hand to press her finger upon the
button of the instrument, and suddenly her arm refuses to obey
her will, and lies numb on the desk beside her. If the tendons of
her wrist had been cut through, her manual helplessness would
not be greater. The strongest voluntary force is too feeble to
make itself felt at the ends of the fingers. The operator simply
can not do her work.[27]

The only known treatment for the affliction was staying off the
key until the symptoms disappeared; Ma Kiley reported that the
telegrapher's cramp she experienced in 1907–1908 after reporting
the Prohibitionist convention "laid me up for a week." In the 1890s,
advertisements for arm braces, which were reputed to alleviate the
condition, began to appear in telegraphic trade magazines.

Working hours depended on the type of office. For railroad
operators, working hours depended on the arrival of trains and
might vary from one day to the next. Commercial operators, however, normally worked fixed shifts, or *tricks*. The typical working
day at a large Western Union office in the 1880s was ten hours;
since the office was in continuous operation, operators took turns
doing evening and Sunday tricks. Evening tricks were shorter,
typically seven and a half hours. No premium was offered for
evening or weekend work; this became an issue in some of the
labor disputes. By the early part of the twentieth century, telegraphers had demanded, and gotten, a 54-hour week for men and a
48-hour week for women. It was this law, referred to as the eight-
hour law for women operators, that the Western Union chief operator asked Ma Kiley to speak against in Sacramento, California, in
1911. She refused, saying later, "Fine thing for a female union
operator to protest a bill that was intended to benefit the
women."[28]

Wages tended to fluctuate greatly based on economic conditions and the local labor supply. In 1905, Ma Kiley made $50 a
month working for Western Union at Del Rio, Texas—a fairly

good salary for a second-class telegrapher with two years' experience, but not enough to raise two children on. In 1911, while working as a first-class operator for Western Union in San Francisco, she made $150 a month, making her probably one of the highest-paid women operators in the country.

During her years with the Southern Pacific Railroad, her monthly salary ranged from a low of $36 in July of 1924 to a high of $125 in September of 1927. As it did with most telegraphers, the Great Depression took its toll on her salary; her average monthly income of around $100 in early 1929 dropped to around $80 a month by mid-1930. Unlike many others, however, she managed to remain employed throughout the worst years of the depression. In December of 1930, 15 percent of Commercial Telegraphers' Union members reported that they were unemployed, and many who were working held only part-time positions. The telegraph companies laid off numerous Morse operators during this period and replaced them with teletype operators at a lower rate of pay. In November 1931, Western Union and Postal Telegraph Company cut the wages of their remaining telegraphers by 10 percent.

By the time Ma Kiley retired in 1942, her salary was $108 a month, a fairly typical salary for a first-class operator. Assuming a 160-hour month, her pay was about 67 cents an hour, above the average of 59 cents an hour for all telegraph operators in June 1941.[29]

In general, in the twentieth century, women telegraphers continued to be paid less than men for the same work It appears that women generally were paid two-thirds to three-quarters of what a man would make for the same work. Ma Kiley experienced this kind of discrimination in 1907 in Austin, Texas. When the manager of the telegraph office told her that he "paid the men sixty-five dollars and the women forty and fifty" she replied that "this woman didn't work for any such salary." By demanding equal pay and sticking to her guns, Ma Kiley managed to stay on a par with her male counterparts salary-wise, something that few of her female contemporaries were able to do.[30]

"That Bug and I Really Went Places."

Why did Ma Kiley become a telegrapher? For the same two reasons that most other women got into the profession— she needed a job and she liked the work.

Most women who got into telegraphy in the nineteenth and early twentieth centuries had several things in common: they came from a working-class or lower-middle-class background, they were intelligent and literate, they had a knack for technology, and they needed an income to support themselves. They often had a family to support as well. In most cases, they did not enter the workplace due to an abstract desire to live an independent life, but rather because of a real need to support themselves financially. Many of them might have echoed the words of Mildred Sunnidale, heroine of telegrapher Josie Schofield's 1875 romance in the *Telegrapher*, "Wooing by Wire": "Although she had been earning her own living, bravely and uncomplainingly, for nearly twelve years, it was not from any desire to be independent that she did so, but simply because she had no one to earn it for her."[31]

In short, they were women who did not follow the traditional nineteenth-century pattern of being supported first by a father and later by a husband. The majority were young women who had not yet married; they tended to enter the field in late adolescence and stay only a few years until they married. Some were from homes where the father was absent or irregularly employed, and were helping to support an extended family. Older women operators tended to be widowed or divorced, though some were married women with living husbands who continued to work full or part time.

For nineteenth- and early twentieth-century women, telegraphy was desirable work. Martha Rayne, in her 1893 book, *What Can a Woman Do?*, gave this description of the work: "It does not soil their dresses; it does not keep them in a standing posture; it does not, they say, compromise them socially. A telegraph operator, they declare, has a social position not inferior to that of a teacher or governess."[32]

It is clear, too, that women got into the field because they enjoyed it; telegraphy was one of the few jobs available to women that involved specialized technical knowledge. Minnie Swan Mitchell, reminiscing in the 1930s about her telegraphic career in the 1880s, wrote, "It meant something in those . . . years, to be a telegraph operator. They were looked upon with wonder as possessing knowledge which separated them from the rest of the crowd."[33] Josie Schofield gives this account of her protagonist's, Mildred Sunnidale's, entry into the work:

> Most of her life had been spent at school teaching in a country town, and wearisome enough she found it, trying to train the minds of her rustic pupils. Anxious for a change, she determined to learn telegraphy, and for this purpose made arrangements with the operator, Mr. Wylie, to instruct her in the mysteries of the art, and let her practice in his office after school hours. She had been practicing most perseveringly for over two years, and was now a pretty fair sound operator, but unfortunately, could not get a situation. After sending in about half a dozen applications, which always met with the same discouraging reply, "No vacancies at present," she began to despair of ever getting an office, and tried to settle down contentedly to school teaching. But she had no taste for it, and found it irksome. With telegraphy it was different. She felt sure she could succeed at that, for her heart was in it. To her there was an interest—a fascination about it. It was so much pleasanter than going over, day after day, and year after year, the same dull lessons, with duller children. It was the height of her ambition to be put in charge of a nice little office of her own.[34]

The key to learning telegraphy for most women was to find a skilled operator to teach them Morse code, and to gain access to a telegraph office where they could read code off the line and observe the operators at work. In some cases, the skilled operator was a woman as well; Mary Macaulay, who would later become a commercial press operator and vice president of the Commercial Telegraphers' Union of America, learned telegraphy at the age of thirteen in 1878 from Mrs. Nellie Chaddock, who was the operator at the railroad depot in Macaulay's hometown of Le Roy, New York.[35]

Entering the profession at the age of thirteen or fourteen was not particularly unusual for either boys or girls. In an age when child labor laws were either nonexistent or weakly enforced, an adolescent who demonstrated persistence and aptitude could volunteer to substitute on an informal basis for the regular operator and eventually acquire a paying position. The stories of Thomas Edison and Andrew Carnegie, who started out in telegraph offices at early ages, are well known. Although not so well remembered, girls like Hattie Huthison, the ten-year-old telegrapher of Brazoria County, Texas, in the early 1880s, and Ellen Laughton, who operated the Dover, New Hampshire, telegraph office in 1852 at the age of fourteen, and became manager of the Portsmouth, New Hampshire, office four years later, were widely written up in nineteenth-century newspapers and popular magazines.[36]

Although Ma Kiley's formal education ended with the fifth grade, her family was able to provide the children with additional private tutoring. Thus she had a fairly good general education for a girl growing up in rural western Texas. Since one of the primary requirements for telegraphy was a high level of literacy, most women who became telegraph operators had a formal public school education. Almost all had a grammar school education, and many were high school graduates. In the late nineteenth century, the number of female high school graduates actually exceeded the number of male graduates; this pool of qualified women provided a source of labor not only for clerical work, as Margery Davies noted in her 1982 study of female office workers, *Woman's Place Is at the Typewriter*, but also for telegraphy.[37]

In addition to primary and secondary education, many telegraphers had additional training, either at a business college that taught telegraphy or at one of the telegraphic schools maintained by the telegraph companies themselves. The commercial telegraph companies had maintained schools since the 1860s to teach women telegraphy; the most noted was the Cooper Institute, jointly run by Cooper Union and Western Union in New York City. (Cooper Union had been established by Peter Cooper in New York City in 1859 to offer free instruction to both men and women in the applied sciences.) The Cooper Institute was founded in 1869; it provided women between the ages of seventeen and twenty-four a four-month-long education under the often stern tutelage of Lizzie Snow, who was not only directress of the institute but also manager of the City Department at Western Union in New York City. During the twenty or so years of the school's existence, it graduated as many as eighty women a year.[38]

Private business and telegraphic colleges also offered courses in telegraphy during the nineteenth and early twentieth centuries; however, they were regarded by operators as "plug factories," and their graduates were held in low esteem. The editor of the *Telegrapher,* writing in 1865, probably echoed the feelings of many operators when he stated, ". . . to teach telegraphing in one of these colleges is like teaching a boy to swim on dry-land; the element is as much lacking in one as the other."[39]

The best way to learn telegraphy was to practice sending and receiving. Like Ma Kiley, many operators rigged up a practice set consisting of a key and a sounder on a wooden board; this enabled them to learn sending and to build up speed. Time spent using a practice set was time well spent, as it increased an operator's chances of qualifying for the more lucrative first-class positions.

Just as important as learning the Morse code and equipment operation was learning the language of the business that was transacted over the lines. Operators who mistook "C.O.D." for "seed" were likely to find themselves singled out for ridicule in the pages of the *Telegrapher*. Women operators were particularly sensitive to this issue, as there were few opportunities for women to learn the language of business in the mid-nineteenth century. Mrs. M. E. Lewis, a New York telegrapher, responding to charges that women did not understand business, replied in the pages of the *Telegrapher* in 1866, "It is men's fault if women do not understand business. If men did right, all women would be taught business enough while at school or afterwards, to fit them for managing their own affairs."[40]

Railroad operators had to learn the obscure language of the railroaders as well, a language in which a mistake could cost money or even human lives. For this, there was no substitute for being at the depot, working with the railroaders and learning their language. Ma Kiley, like many others, approached this step indirectly, first being allowed to copy code in the stationmaster's office before being allowed into the telegrapher's office.

Ma Kiley's Scotch-Irish ancestry was typical of telegraphers. Most telegraphers in the early years tended to be native-born Americans with English-speaking ancestry. This was due primarily to the need for proficiency in written and spoken English. Later, other immigrant groups began to see telegraphy as a means of gaining entry into the American middle class. Among the women, a high percentage were Irish; this was probably due to both the relatively high degree of literacy of the Irish when compared with other recent immigrants, and the tendency of Irish women to marry later in life and thus spend more time in the workforce. Edwin Gabler, in his 1988 social history, *The American Telegrapher*, found that of seventy women operators in New York City in 1880, 71 percent were of Irish ancestry.[41]

At least in terms of ethnicity, the profession was relatively nondiscriminatory. At the 1865 convention of the National Telegraphers' Union, where the admission of women to the profession was debated, it was noted without surprise that there were several African-American men working as telegraphers in the South. In the 1870s, the Cuban-American brothers, Ambrose and Narciso Gonzales, had begun telegraphic careers in South Carolina that would eventually result in the founding of the *Columbia (S.C.) State*, the progressive newspaper they edited. By 1900, names of all ethnic derivations began to appear in the telegraphic journals, and a few African-American women were listed in that year's census as telegraph operators.[42]

It is difficult to say exactly what percentage of telegraph operators were women. Ma Kiley's perception of telegraphy, especially
railroad telegraphy, as being largely a man's world is correct.
Women were always in the minority and had to fight for recognition and equal treatment. The first census to differentiate occupations by sex was that of 1870; in it, 355, or 4 percent of the total of
8,316 telegraphers, were reported to be women. By 1920, the year
in which the census reported the largest number of telegraphers,
16,860, or 21.2 percent of the total of 79,434, were women. As the
number of telegraphers declined during the 1930s and 1940s, the
percentage of women remained about the same; in the 1940 census,
8228, or 20.7 percent of the total of 39,782, were women.

However, census figures, especially in the nineteenth century,
were not always accurate, and women workers in particular were
likely to be underrepresented. While it is difficult to establish
exactly what percentage of telegraphers were women, it is even
more difficult to determine what percentage of telegraphers were
railroad operators, as opposed to commercial operators. Telegraphers, female as well as male, were often boomers who moved frequently from job to job, in search of higher pay or just a change of
scenery; they also frequently changed from railroad jobs to commercial jobs, or the reverse, based on which office offered the best
opportunity. The telegraphers' strikes in 1870, 1883, and 1907 created a mass exodus from commercial offices to railroad depots;
some operators were blacklisted by Western Union and the other
commercial companies, and others simply refused to sign the iron-
clad oaths required by the commercial companies in order to qualify for reinstatement. Archibald McIsaac, in his 1933 study of railroad telegraphers, estimated that in the 1880s, about two-thirds of
all telegraphers worked for the railroads, a figure that probably
remained valid until the 1920s.[43]

"Word Got About That There Was a Woman in the Office."

Telegraphers in general enjoyed a rich and varied social life in the nineteenth and early twentieth centuries, including enthusiastic attendance at concerts, dances, and the theater. Although such outings provided an opportunity for romance, the easiest way to meet an eligible someone of the opposite sex was by means of the telegraph itself. In fact, the telegraph played an important role in the social lives of most telegraphers. One way in which telegraphers can be seen as modern is in their use of the telegraph as an early form of electronic mail, to stay in touch with one another and exchange information on jobs. Many romances began with casual after-hours exchanges of personal messages over the telegraph line. Ma Kiley met at least one of her husbands, Alexander John Crew, over the line, and renewed her acquaintance with Albert Kuhn telegraphically after a thirty-five-year hiatus. This phenomenon even created its own genre of popular literature, the "telegraphic romance."

The stories began to appear in popular magazines around 1870, at a time when Western Union, the industry giant, began to actively recruit women into the profession. One of the first telegraphic romances to appear in print was Justin McCarthy's "Along the Wires," which appeared in the February 1870 issue of *Harper's New Monthly Magazine*. It is the story of Annette Langley, a telegraph operator in a large telegraph office in "one of the great Atlantic cities," and her romance with one of her customers, Dr. Childers.[44]

Barnet Phillips's "The Thorsdale Telegraphs," a telegraphic romance that appeared in the October 1876 *Atlantic Monthly*, deals with the issue of women operators in the railroad depot. It is the first-person story of Mary Brown, age nineteen, who has just graduated from a business college where she studied telegraphy. She is offered a job by the railroad, which sends her to the desolate Midwestern town of Thorsdale, where she undergoes a series of adventures before falling in love with Jahn Thor, the stationmaster.[45]

Not surprisingly, many of the authors of telegraphic romances were women telegraphers themselves. Many saw an opportunity to use their writing skills to weave a plot out of their everyday experiences at the telegraph office. Lida A. Churchill wrote a novel called *My Girls*, based on her experiences as an operator at Northbridge, Massachusetts, in 1882. It portrayed the lives and experiences of a group of women telegraphers who found both successful careers and romance in New York City; it provided such a positive image of the occupation that the editors of the *Operator*, another telegraphers' trade journal, felt prompted to insert the following warning in a review of the book: "We hope that no girl operators will be led by the glowing pictures that are given of the success of the heroines to think of following their example by going to New York. In this respect the story is extremely improbable, and might do harm."[46]

"Jo," from Toronto, Canada, already familiar to readers of the *Telegrapher* for her witty and down-to-earth letters, wrote a romance entitled "Wooing by Wire" that appeared first in the *New Dominion* of Hamilton, Ontario, and later in the *Telegrapher* in November 1875. Jo was actually Josie Schofield, the only woman operator at the Toronto office of the Dominion Telegraph Company in 1875.[47]

"Wooing by Wire" is the story of Mildred Sunnidale, a self-described "old maid" of thirty. She has been self-supporting for twelve years, first as a schoolteacher and then as a telegrapher; her parents and other close relatives have long since died. She makes the telegraphic acquaintance of Tom Gordon, the operator at the next station down the line. After a series of comic misunderstandings, the two fall in love and are engaged to be married.

Of the three stories, only "Wooing by Wire" discusses the issue of women in the telegraph office, and how they were perceived by their male co-workers, from the point of view of the operator herself. While McCarthy's character, Annette, has no thoughts about her presence in a male-dominated field, and Phillips's Mary Brown concludes that she has no place in the telegraph office, Jo Schofield's Mildred simply gives notice that she is here, and that

the men should accustom themselves to it; her self-confident attitude is attributable in part to the steadily increasing numbers of
women in telegraphy by the mid-1870s.

Jo's story reflects the conventional view that, for most women
of the age, marriage and family were the primary goals; but there
is a subtext that says that having a fulfilling professional career is
not incompatible with marriage and family. If one undertakes a
career, the story makes clear, it should be challenging and fulfilling
in and of itself. Readers of the *Telegrapher* were already aware of
Jo's views on the subject from her earlier letters to the journal:

> The grand thing for girls, as well as for men, is to find some-
> thing to do, and then do it heartily. As Carlyle says, "An endless
> significance lies in work: in idleness alone there is perpetual
> despair." It is surely far better for us to be engaged in some use-
> ful business, earning our own living and making the most of our
> abilities, than to sit idly with folded hands waiting for the "com-
> ing man," who is often so long in coming and worth so little
> when he arrives.[48]

It is intriguing to speculate on the effect that the telegraphic
romance genre had on patterns of courtship, both among telegraphers and among the general public. Probably one direct effect was
the sudden popularity of marriage by telegraph in the late 1870s. One
such marriage occurred in 1876 when G. Scott Jeffreys, the Western
Union operator at Waynesburg, Pennsylvania, and Lida Culler, the
telegrapher at Brownsville, Pennsylvania, were wed by telegraph
after a courtship that began over the wires. The couple stood at the
Brownsville office, together with wedding retinue, while the minis-
ter officiated by telegraph from the Waynesburg office. The complete text of the wedding service, including the "I do's" telegraphed
by the bride and groom, was printed in the *Telegrapher*.[49]

Marriage by telegraph became such a fad that the *New York
Times* felt compelled to question its legality in an editorial in 1884.
While admitting that the legality of a marriage by telegraph had
never been tested by the courts, the *Times* opined that "ministers

who lend themselves to such a mockery of law and morality as a marriage by telegraph . . . are lending their aid to enable foolish people to live in a state of concubinage."[50]

Women telegraph operators were featured in the movies as well. Some of D. W. Griffith's earliest full-length silent films were about women telegraphers, including *The Lonedale Operator* (1911), starring Blanche Sweet, and *The Girl and Her Trust* (1912), starring Dorothy Bernard. *The Girl and Her Trust* is the story of Grace, a telegraph operator at a remote railroad station in the West, who is assigned the task of guarding a mining company payroll. She rejects the advances of the station agent, who leaves in dejection. She then must watch over the chest of money alone. Two desperados break into the station and attempt to steal the payroll; she barricades herself in the telegraph office and desperately sends off a plea for help, just before one of the robbers cuts the line. She fools the robbers into believing that she has a gun by exploding a bullet in the keyhole with a screwdriver and hammer. The robbers then depart with the payroll on a handcar, in hopes of breaking the chest open. She rushes out of the office and jumps on the handcar in a vain attempt to stop the robbery. Just as the villains have subdued her and are about to throw her off the handcar, a train arrives. It is full of railroad men, sent by the telegrapher at the next station in response to her telegraphic plea for help.

The film is innovative in a number of ways. It is one of the earliest movies to employ a moving camera; the train chase scenes appear to be shot from a moving vehicle. It is also unusual in that it portrays a woman as the central character, playing an active role.

As the western developed as a genre, female telegraphers occasionally appeared as stock characters, though generally in passive roles where they provided romantic interest. Virginia Gilmore portrays telegrapher Sue Creighton in *Western Union* (1941); as the men set off westward to build the Transcontinental Telegraph line, she remarks wistfully that she wishes she could have been born a man so that she could go along. Gail Davis plays a stronger role in the Tim Holt western, *Overland Telegraph* (1951), as Colleen

Muldoon, a telegrapher and line stringer who takes over management of her father's telegraph company after he is killed by outlaws. In *Kansas Pacific* (1953), Eve Miller plays Barbara Bruce, the daughter of a section chief who battles Confederate saboteurs as he builds the Kansas Pacific Railroad in pre–Civil War Kansas; her telegraphic skills make her the only link between the isolated railroad construction camp and the rest of the world.

"Your Operator Showed Up with a Dress On."

Although the telegraphic romances reflected the increased acceptance of women in a nontraditional workplace, overt discrimination, lower pay, and sexual harassment were part of the reality of life in the depot telegraph office for many female operators. "Partly because of the prejudice against hiring women," Ma Kiley observed, "there were times when the only 'operating' I could do was with a mop or broom."[51]

It was an issue that first began to be publicly discussed in the late 1860s. As the Civil War drew to an end and the men began to return home, competition for jobs arose. Women operators had come to view themselves as technical professionals and were unwilling to abandon the skills they had acquired to return to more traditional domestic roles. Also, many had become their family's sole breadwinner due to the loss of a husband or father. A debate arose in the pages of the *Telegrapher*, the leading trade journal, over the role of women in the telegraph industry, the tone of which seems modern and confrontational even today, more than a century after the fact.

In the second issue of the *Telegrapher* (31 October 1864), a female operator, who signed her letter "Susannah," wrote in to ask if the telegraphers' labor organization, the National Telegraphic Union, would admit women as members. Susannah's request precipitated a debate between male operators, who questioned the skills of female telegraphers, and the women operators themselves, who rebutted the men's arguments, often angrily.[52]

In the 26 December 1864 issue, a letter from "T. A.," a male operator, raised the gender issue that was of greatest significance to the male operators—the threat of women taking jobs away from men. He pointed out that the American Telegraph Company, under the leadership of General Marshall K. Lefferts, was training women in Morse telegraphy free of charge, in hopes of employing them in its offices. Since women would work for a lower wage than men, he alleged, they would eventually replace men in the telegraph office. He concluded, "What operators should do to protect themselves from 'hard times' is to keep the ladies out of the National Telegraphic Union, and also as much as possible off the lines."[53]

T. A.'s comments escalated the level of the debate. His letter received an angry response from "Magnetta" in the 27 February 1865 issue, in which she accused him of hypocrisy and selfishness:

> But how I shudder as I imagine your mother at home washing your linen, while your sister blacks your boots!
>
> If I have brought "hard times" to your door by being allowed on the lines, I earnestly wish your soul may find ample field for expansion, and you be promoted to message boy, with a salary of fifty cents per day![54]

There was much debate in the 1870s over whether or not it was appropriate to place women in railroad telegraph offices, where they would have to deal with violence, drunkenness, and profanity. In the 9 January 1875 issue of the *Telegrapher*, a male operator using the pseudonym, "Nihil Nameless," attempted to point out the vicissitudes that a female operator would have to endure in the railroad depot, under the heading "Will the Coming Operator Be a Woman?":

> When Miss A____ has learned the business, she must get a situation. . . . She cannot afford to wait until one is offered, acceptable

in every way. She must take such as she can get. Suppose that happened to be at the stock yards, or at a railroad repairing shop, such as I have seen, her office will be surrounded, perhaps thronged with men of the rudest, most uncultured type, glaring on her through her window, asking her impertinent or insulting questions and giving utterance to the most shocking profanity. She must bear it; she cannot protect herself, nor punish the offenders. . . . an accident occurs out on the railroad over which her line runs, she must go in the night and the storm, perhaps, and attach the instrument to the wires, and sitting there alone and unprotected, among blasphemous men, work while chilling rain drenches her, freezing as it falls.[55]

In the 23 January issue, a female operator, "Aliquae," responded to his letter:

One who is naturally refined will not lose her identity by coming in contact with others. And one who respects herself, will always be respected.

And is it any worse to hand orders, etc., to a few workmen, than to give orders to the butcher, the baker, etc., at home? A woman cannot stay forever penned up at home, and only go out into the world hemmed in by a father or a brother on one side and a husband on the other.[56]

In contrast with the situation of ten years before, "Nihil Nameless" found few supporters of his own sex. In fact, this round of discussion was effectively closed by one "John Sterling," who wrote in the 27 March 1875 issue, "Lady operators are an established fact, and whatever may be our views of the 'sphere of woman,' we may as well accept the situation, and drop *that* subject."[57]

Although female operators were indeed an established fact by the mid-1870s, this did not mean that male operators were comfortable with their presence in the telegraph office. For many men of the age, allowing women to live independently and compete on an equal basis constituted a threat to the moral fiber of society. One writer complained in *Electric Age* in 1887 that allowing women equal footing in the telegraph office, "if followed to its legitimate conclusion, will break up the marriage state and result in what? community life, polygamous life, or barbarous life."[58]

In her 1993 essay on Atlanta telegrapher O. Delight Smith, historian Jacqueline Dowd Hall remarked, "As featured in dime novels and union journals, they [women telegraphers] were notable less for their skills than for their unsupervised sexuality." This reflects a general perception that female telegraphers were somehow more knowing and worldly, particularly regarding sexual matters, than their more sheltered sisters who did not venture out into the workaday world. On one level, this belief was sublimated into the telegraphic romance view of telegraph operators as being available for romantic involvement; on another level, it sometimes resulted in accusations of promiscuity. Ma Kiley encountered such a problem in Baker, Montana, in 1908, when she filed a slander suit against a station agent who made "slurring remarks" against her character.[59]

One source of this perception was the operating environment of the railroad telegrapher. The railroad station in the late nineteenth century was located at the exact edge of respectable middle-class society; while it was a place where businessmen and even their wives and children might venture safely, it was also a place where they would encounter persons from vastly different levels of society, including common workmen, drunkards, gamblers, and prostitutes. Even today, when we speak of someone as coming from "the wrong side of the tracks," we are invoking the railroad depot symbolically as a point of social demarcation.

In many small towns, houses of prostitution were located near the railroad depot for the convenience of traveling salesmen and other itinerant men who frequented them. "Railroad hotel" became a common euphemism for such an establishment. Ma Kiley noted that a house of prostitution and a saloon were directly across the tracks from the railroad depot at Baker, Montana, when she worked there in 1908; it was, she said, the first time she had ever seen "women of that reputation."

At any rate, women telegraphers working in railroad depots certainly knew of these places in the vicinity of railroad depots, and knew what went on in them. It was the sort of knowledge of the world and its evil ways from which patriarchal society tried to shield women; female telegraphers were seen as being in danger of moral corruption simply by possessing this knowledge.

Anxieties about the corrupting influence of the working environment of women telegraphers were expressed by women reformers as well as by men. Writing to her sister, Mary, in 1907, Margaret Dreier Robins, president of the National Women's Trade Union League, claimed that a combination of low wages and the "easy tolerance" shown by some women operators toward the "sporting element" that frequented their offices had led them into the "red light district":

> The young woman is acting as a public official, and she must, therefore, send messages even when they are accompanied by familiar attentions often forced upon her by the so called "sporting element" found at these public places. It is surely intolerable that she should find herself in her ordinary day's work in a position where she cannot rightfully resent such acts, and where her wage is dependent on the toleration she shows.
>
> We have known of some tragic instances where some of these same girls got into the "red light district" through the easy toleration they showed.

However, she added that she did not wish to discuss the issue publicly, as she felt it would reflect on the character of women operators in general.[60]

A case that attracted much public attention was that of Maggie McCutcheon, a twenty-year-old telegrapher in Brooklyn in 1886. The story appeared in *Electrical World* under the heading, "The Dangers of Wired Love," a reference to a popular telegraphic romance, *Wired Love*:

> George W. McCutcheon, of 1204 Fulton Street, Brooklyn, has a daughter, Maggie, 20 years of age, whose ability to use a Morse

> telegraph instrument brought him into Justice Kenna's court,
> last week on a charge of threatening to blow her brains out. . . .
> Maggie was an expert telegrapher, made his store a local station,
> and had an instrument put in one corner. . . . He soon found
> out however, that Miss Maggie was always communicating with
> men at different points on the wire, and keeping up a flirtation.

Maggie became telegraphically acquainted with a Frank Frisbie,
a telegrapher with the Long Island Railroad. After the two telegraphers had met several times, Maggie's father became suspicious
and made some inquiries. He discovered that Frisbie was a married man with a family in Pennsylvania; he forbade his daughter to
see Frisbie again, even sending her away to the Catskill Mountains
in order to end the liaison. When Maggie returned, she applied to
the manager of Western Union and resumed work as a telegrapher at 599 Bedford Avenue, where she could escape the watchful
eye of her father. She also resumed the liaison with Frisbie, arrang-
ing to meet him at a house on Graham Avenue.

> One Sunday evening, Mr. McCutcheon returned to his home to
> be told that Maggie had gone to the house in Graham Avenue
> where she formerly met Frisbie, and was not to return that
> evening. He started to bring her home and succeeded, but his
> daughter alleges that he threatened to blow her brains out, and
> she therefore had him arrested.[61]

Clearly Maggie was behaving in a way that went against the
grain of late Victorian America, with her actions spelling danger
to the male-dominated world of 1886. Her story reflects the
unique situation of women telegraphers in the latter part of the
nineteenth century. Because of their profession, they commanded
an income that permitted independent living and the ability to
change employers at will; their telegraphic skills also allowed
them to communicate with whomever they chose, without the
chaperoning or censorship provided by parents and family. Thus,
they were able, in a sense, to step outside of the patriarchal

society at will, if they so desired. It is this ability to step in and out of the social bounds of their time that makes them seem so contemporary to us, and so atypical—even dangerous—to their contemporaries.

"I Never Did and Never Would Scab."

Ma Kiley was a dedicated union member. Having joined the Order of Railroad Telegraphers in 1903, she never wavered in her support of the union: "That pin, and my union card, enabled me to travel many a mile on the railroads without paying a cent; and there were times when, without it, I would have gone jobless and hungry." There came times, as in San Francisco in 1911, when she had no choice but to take off her union pin in order to find work, but she never abandoned the principles that it represented to her.[62]

Telegraphers in general were ambiguous about their class status, alternating between a desire for middle-class respectability and working-class solidarity. As Edwin Gabler noted in *The American Telegrapher,* their upwardly mobile dress and clean, uncalloused hands caused members of the traditional craft unions, such as pipefitters and ironworkers, to speak of telegraphers disdainfully as "kid-gloved laborers." Telegraphers first began to organize labor movements during the Civil War as a means of improving working conditions and maintaining the high wage levels they had become accustomed to during the war. However, the first nationwide strike did not take place until 1870, when the Telegraphers' Protective League, a secretive organization that required members to take an oath of loyalty and used cipher codes to transmit messages over the lines, called operators out for a disastrous fifteen-day strike to protest a cut in wages at the San Francisco Western Union office. The strike failed to achieve any of its goals, and the telegraph companies simply brought in strikebreakers.[63]

The next major strike occurred in 1883, when the Brotherhood of Telegraphers, formed as part of the Knights of Labor,
struck for higher pay, shorter hours, and an end to the "sliding
scale" system in which a telegrapher would be hired at a rate
slightly less than what his or her predecessor received for the same
work. It was the first telegraphers' organization to have an agenda
related to women: it supported equal pay for equal work. However, the strike was poorly planned and the union did not have
sufficient funding for a long strike; the walkout ended after
approximately one month. The Brotherhood of Telegraphers
ceased to exist after the strike, and it would be many years before
commercial telegraphers again attempted to organize a union.[64]

The Order of Railway Telegraphers was founded in Cedar
Rapids, Iowa, in 1886; it was the first union formed specifically to
address the needs of railroad operators. (The name was changed to
the Order of Railroad Telegraphers in 1891.) In fact, the ORT was
ideologically closer to the conservative railroad unions, such as the
Brotherhood of Locomotive Engineers, than to the more militant
commercial telegraphers. As part of the reaction to the abortive
strikes of 1870 and 1883, it even had a clause in its articles of association that forbade strikes except under extreme conditions. By
1903, when Ma Kiley joined, the union boasted a membership of
around twenty thousand, which constituted perhaps half of the
railroad telegraphers in the United States. The ORT functioned
primarily as a benevolent organization that paid benefits to out-of-
work members and helped them to find work.[65]

Around the turn of the century, the commercial operators
began to form labor organizations again. The Commercial Telegraphers Union of America was formed in 1902 as an offshoot of
the ORT for the specific purpose of organizing commercial operators. Its stated goal was to gain membership among Western
Union employees, and to eventually represent Western Union
telegraphers in negotiations with the telegraph company. By this
time, there were only two large commercial telegraph companies,
Western Union and Postal Telegraph Company, who between

them monopolized the telegraph business in the United States. The CTUA had ten thousand members by 1904.[66]

By the beginning of 1907, discontent was spreading among telegraphers and it was clear that a strike was a possible outcome. The issues were similar to those that precipitated previous strikes—low pay, long working hours, bad working conditions. In Chicago in 1907, pay rates for telegraphers ranged from $25.00 to $82.50 a month. Working hours were typically ten hours a day, six days a week, with frequent Sunday work as well, in operating rooms that were often poorly lighted and ventilated. Three-quarters of women operators made less than $45.00 a month. Pay rates had not increased since the 1880s, while buying power had gone down. Wages were actually numerically lower than they had been during the 1860s.[67]

Another issue that was causing discontent among operators was the cost of providing a typewriter. In many offices, operators had to provide typewriters at their own expense. Elizabeth Butler, writing in *Women and the Trades* in 1909, made these observations:

> The typewriter is part of the operator's equipment. When it was first introduced, a special bonus was offered to employees who would learn to use it, and as its use became general, it proved as valuable to the employees as to the company. Many whose handwriting was poor, and who on this account had been classed below first-class, were able to draw higher pay. Operators, however, are required to buy and to keep in repair their own machines, which is a heavy initial purchase.

Butler also noted that the sliding scale was being used primarily to replace men with women at a lower rate of pay in 1907.

> But important as these points were, abolition of the sliding scale was the cardinal demand. The grievance referred to as the "sliding scale" was the outcome of alleged differences in the work done by men and by women, and of resultant unfair discrimination. . . .

Although the work might tell on women sooner than on men, and although they might in some cases be less efficient than men, they were yet sufficiently capable to supersede men at a lower rate of pay. They were lending themselves to a scheme for cutting wages.[68]

Union activities among its operators had begun to draw the attention of Western Union by early 1907. If CTUA members wore their union buttons to work, Western Union managers would ask them to remove them, and, in some cases, fire them for refusing to do so. In May 1907, the CTUA drew up a list of grievances and presented it to R. C. Clowry, president of Western Union, charging that the company had failed to live up to its earlier promise of a 10 percent raise and was summarily dismissing employees for wearing union buttons.[69]

In June 1907, operators in San Francisco went on strike after a request for a temporary, 25 percent pay increase (to cover additional living expenses caused by the San Francisco earthquake) was turned down by Western Union. CTUA officials began to negotiate a settlement with Charles P. Neill of the U.S. Labor Bureau, who served as intermediary in discussions with Western Union, which did not recognize the union. By 19 July, an agreement was reached that would have given all telegraphers a 10-percent raise, and that would have guaranteed the San Francisco strikers reinstatement when they returned to work. The San Francisco local of the CTUA voted to accept these terms and return to work.[70]

However, events occurred shortly thereafter that dashed hopes of a negotiated settlement. During the San Francisco strike, Mrs. Sadie Nichols, a nonunion beginning operator in San Francisco, was put on the wire to Los Angeles, a position normally reserved for first-class operators, as a reward for not joining the strike. The union operators in Los Angeles learned that she had been a "scab" during the strike, and began to harass her. Operator Paddy Ryan in Los Angeles refused to work with Sadie Nichols and told her over the line that "the place for her to live was in a notorious bawdy house in San Francisco." She in turn called Ryan a "liar."

She reported Ryan to management on 23 July, and he was fired after being taped and it was proven that her accusations were correct. (Being *taped* meant that management put a recording telegraph on an operator's line to determine exactly what was being sent and received.) On 7 August, operators in Los Angeles went on strike to show their support of Ryan.[71]

Women operators had the choice of viewing the incident in California as a women's issue or as a labor issue. Most seemed to side with the union and to blame Western Union for placing Mrs. Nichols in a position for which she was not qualified. In Chicago, operators went on strike on 9 August, refusing to work with the nonunion operator in Los Angeles who had replaced Ryan. At this point, the CTUA, presented with a fait accompli by the rank and file, had no choice but to authorize the strike on 15 August. Meanwhile, the ORT had ordered members to refuse Western Union traffic on 11 August; on the same day, Associated Press operators struck for higher pay. All told, between ten thousand and fifteen thousand operators struck across the country during the summer of 1907.[72]

More than any of the previous strikes, the strike of 1907 brought the issues of the women operators into focus. Female strike leaders emerged, such as Mrs. Louise Forcey, who led the striking operators out of Postal Telegraph Company in Chicago, and Hilda Svenson, who became a strike leader in New York. Margaret Dreier Robins of the National Women's Trade Union League spoke in support of the strikers, and a committee was set up to coordinate the actions of the NWTUL and the female members of the CTUA. One significant outcome of this collaboration was an open letter to Helen Gould, daughter of financier Jay Gould and a major stockholder in Western Union, listing the reasons why the women operators were taking part in the strike and asking for her support. Although Helen Gould was known to be sympathetic to women's issues, it appears that the letter had little effect on the outcome of the strike.[73]

In New York City, Rose Pastor Stokes, the Socialist orator, addressed the striking telegraphers. The former cigar wrapper, whose unlikely odyssey from the slums of Cleveland to marriage into one of America's wealthiest families made her one of the best-known women of the age, delivered a speech on 25 August 1907, citing the unfairness of companies in requiring telegraphers to furnish their own typewriters: "An eight-hour day must be believed in by all fair-minded people both among the workers and the employers. As long as the company believes you can buy your own typewriters it will insist on your buying them and take the profits for your work. It was so with us in the cigar trade and it is so in all trades in which hand tools are used."[74] However, as with earlier strikes, the CTUA strike of 1907 was doomed to failure by a lack of planning and lack of sufficient funding for a protracted strike. Strikers slowly gave up and returned to work, or, as in the earlier strikes, became railroad operators. Finally, on 9 November 1907, the strike was officially called off.[75]

The 1907 strike was, both literally and metaphorically, the third strike for the telegraphers. All had failed for essentially the same reasons: (1) lack of an adequate strike fund, (2) lack of advance planning or forethought, and (3) failure to consider the financial strength of the telegraph companies. Although telegraphers would strike again, on a smaller scale, in 1919 and 1929, the 1907 strike was the last time that a nationwide shutdown of the telegraphic system was used in an attempt to win concessions from the telegraph companies.

Although the strike did not achieve its objectives, women operators in particular did obtain some improvements in their working conditions in the aftermath of the strike. Working hours for women were shortened as a result of congressional inquiry. Although Western Union did not grant any pay increases, its chief competitor, Postal Telegraph Company, gave its employees a 10-percent raise after the strike. Increased numbers of women were hired in 1908, partly to replace men who were not rehired after the strike. And, ironically, working conditions improved in 1909, not in response to the strikers' grievances, but as a result of more efficient management brought about by the merger of

American Telephone and Telegraph Company with Western Union, which lasted until 1913.[76]

For some women participants, the strike brought new visibility and new roles. Hilda Svenson became a professional organizer for the NWTUL. Mary Macaulay used the experience she gained as vice president of Buffalo CTUA Local 41 to become international vice president of the CTUA in 1919. And in Atlanta, Georgia, O. Delight Smith became a journalist for a local labor newspaper, the *Journal of Labor*, after being blacklisted by Western Union for her union activities.[77]

For Ma Kiley, sticking to her principles cost her a job during the strike of 1907, "the only time in my life," as she recalled, that she was actually fired. Working as a railroad operator for the Chicago, Rock Island, and Pacific line in Waurika, Oklahoma, she was obligated as an ORT member to refuse to send any Western Union messages over the line during the strike. When a group of men first tried to bribe her, and then to coerce her into sending a telegram, she replied, "I AM NOT SENDING THAT MESSAGE!" One of the men reported her to railroad authorities, and she was summoned to railroad headquarters in Fort Worth and fired.[78]

The Bug and I

By "Ma Kiley"
(Mattie C. Kuhn)

Copyright © 1950 by *Railroad Magazine*

(Annotated by Thomas C. Jepsen)

PART ONE

I am not trying to be original when I call this story of my life "The Bug And I." It's just my way of saying thanks to that popular book "The Egg And I," for first putting the idea in my head that I, too, had a story of a partnership to tell.

My partner was a "bug." Not one of those live creatures that scare the everlasting daylights out of squeamish, nervous females— but the railroad telegrapher's nickname for a *Vibroplex*, or sending machine.[1] That bug and I really went places. It enabled me to become what was termed a first-class Morse telegrapher, on the railroads and for the Western Union, something that soon will be alive in memory only because the teletype and other machines have put us on the shelf.[2]

Any schoolkid can practice up on a teletype and secure a job that pays top wages, in just a few weeks or months. But to learn the good old Morse takes about a year's time. That's how long it took me, though I do not profess to be very smart. I've heard telegraphers say, "Oh, I learned it in two or three months!" But they were mistaken; they never did learn it. They may have learned to send—anyone can do that—but sending is only about one-third of the game.

Before I was allowed to take my first job I had to know the switchboard, how to ground wires, patch them, trace trouble, etc.[3] Just ask a teletype operator to do that, or for that matter 95 percent of the new Morse telegraphers.

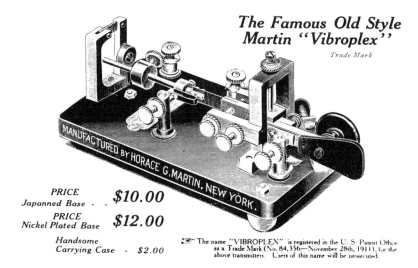

*The Famous Old Style
Martin "Vibroplex"*

Trade Mark

PRICE
Japanned Base - - $10.00

PRICE
Nickel Plated Base $12.00

Handsome
Carrying Case - $2.00

The name "VIBROPLEX" is registered in the U. S. Patent Office
as a Trade Mark (No. 84,356—November 28th, 1911), for the
above transmitters. Users of this name will be prosecuted.

Figure 1. A Vibroplex "bug" or automatic sending key used by telegraphers. Manufactured by Horace G. Martin of New York City. From a Horace G. Martin advertisement, Telegraph and Telephone Age, *1 February 1913, 93.*

So that my readers may recognize me and know that this story is true, guess I'd better turn egg for a while and tell when and where I was hatched.

I'm strictly a country gal of Scotch-Irish descent, American born. A beau I had in Gerlach, Nevada, way back in 1911, once asked me what my "nationality" was. When I told him, Scotch-Irish, American-born, he replied, "By G—, I thought so—you're too damned mean to be plain Irish!"

Anyway I was born down in Atacosa [sic] County, Texas,[4] where the jiggers (redbugs) delight in burying their poisonous selves into your flesh and where the grass burrs scratch the hide off your legs. I arrived on the morning of March 1, 1880, the fourth child in our family.

My mother and dad were divorced when I was about seven years old. The court awarded us kids to mother—William, my oldest brother, myself, my sister Bennie and baby brother Dan, who was a little past two years of age. Mother placed Bennie and me with a sister of hers who lived on the Medina River at a place called Oak Island, about ten miles south of San Antonio. Mother took the youngest child, Dan, with her and went to San Antonio, where she was soon married to one of the finest men who ever drew the breath of life—Daniel G. Franks, a widower and the father of six children. They moved out to Dryden in Pecos County, Texas, where my new daddy was boss of the Pecos Land and Cattle Company, on what was then the Swinging H Ranch.

My own father hated any and all of my mother's people, and as soon as he found out where she had placed us he came and took Bennie and me away with him back to Atacosa County. But he had no home, and as usual no work and no money, so for a long time he put us out with any family who would keep us, free of charge, until his marriage to Texanna Holder, a lovely young woman hardly older than my brother, Will.

We stayed with my dad and my stepmother for about two years, and then in 1891 my own mother came to take me and my sister Bennie to live with her and her new husband, Daniel Franks. As I've said, he had six children of his own, by his former wife, and mother decided that she might as well have hers with her, too. I never did know all the ins and outs of the case, but I remember when we were taken into court. I had on a checked gingham dress, wore a corset underneath, and was barefoot, with my hair in two pigtails "platted" so tight I couldn't close my eyes.

When the judge asked us to state our choice as to which parent we wanted to live with, Bennie immediately replied, "Mamma"; but I answered, "It doesn't make a damn bit of difference to me—I don't like either one of them!" At this time my sister and I were both very ornery, disobedient little hellions; we had no real love for anyone and distrusted almost everyone.

After mother got possession of us she took us to Dryden where we met the whole family. And what a family! There was Daddy Franks, my stepfather, his oldest son, Alonzo, his twin daughters, Arrie Doak and Artie Neale (the latter was married to my first cousin, Henry Neale), Leila Heard, Oscar Franks and Dannie

Franks. Then there was my youngest brother, Dan, and mother's and Daddy Frank's first offspring, Alva, aged two, the idol of all the children. Eleven kids, three distinct sets: "yours, mine, and ours."

Daddy Franks called us all together and said, "Children, we are a big family and I hope a happy one. There is room and welcome for each and every one of you. I want it distinctly understood that there sits the boss"—he pointed to mother—"and I insist that you all respect and obey her. As long as you do, this is your home, but to the first one who breaks that rule—there is the door leading out." That rule stood and the only one who ever got the door was his own son, Alonzo. I can't remember what it was about.

For the first time in my eleven years I had a real home, with affection and understanding. Before retiring we kissed each member of the family and did the same on arising. Dan Franks was the grandest man I ever knew and I have never allowed anyone to even intimate differently, in my presence. He was kind, just, upright, honest and—just 100 percent to the good in every way. He gave me the first doll I ever had. (Before my toys had always consisted of marbles, pocket knives, slingshots, nigger shooters,[5] etc.) This doll stood alone and would close its eyes and say mama. I made clothes for it from scraps Daddy brought me from millinery stores, and he complimented everything I made, when in other years all I ever heard was jibes and ridicule.

At Dryden Daddy Franks was, as I have stated before, boss of the Pecos Land and Cattle Company. He was paid a good salary and allowed his expenses. Mother ran a boardinghouse and collected board from him, which we kids couldn't understand. We thought he was being imposed on. Her other boarders were railroad men Charles Douglas and James Whitely, the day and night pumpers, the agent, Pete Jungman, and Albert Kuhn, the night operator.[6] Now and then a transient would drop in, usually a rancher. You will hear more of Albert Kuhn, and the part he played in my life many years later.

*Figure 2. The combined Franks and Brite families, taken
in front of the Dolch Hotel, Eagle Pass, Texas, around 1895.
This photo appeared in the original* Railroad Magazine *article
under the heading "Buttons and Bows in 1895."*
(Railroad Magazine, *April 1950, 59).*
*Mattie Brite, aged fifteen, stands second from left; her sister, Bennie,
thirteen years old, stands fifth from left.
Seated at right is their mother, Alva; seated next to her is
her husband, Daniel Franks, with their youngest child, Robert, on his lap.
Seated next to him, second from left, is Edward Sturges.
Mattie Kuhn wrote of him in 1949 that
"he had been my very first sweetheart and
we were engaged but Mother broke us up."
(Photograph and identifications courtesy of Bennie Lou Weaver.)*

Because there was no public school where we lived we had a governess, a little woman from Goliad, Texas, by the name of Kate Hatcher. She had all it takes to make a successful teacher and adviser of young children but was growing old and feeble and when the second term came around we were unable to get our dear Miss Kate. Daddy and mother decided they would have to arrange things differently in order to school us younger kids so they bought a place in Del Rio, a 14-acre fruit farm. There we had peaches, plums, apricots, a cork tree, bananas, and gosh only knows what else. After dark we used to bathe in the irrigation ditch, in the bathing suits we brought into the world with us. That place was really a home—we had jersey cows, pigs, chickens and a horse, a big gray rascal that bit anyone coming close to his head.

After two years at Del Rio we leased the fruit farm and went to Eagle Pass where Daddy Franks and mother ran the Dolch Hotel for two years. We lived right near the Rio Grande River, the bridge to Mexico being only about five blocks from the hotel. On Thursday and Sunday nights there was always a band concert, given by the Eagle Pass band, at the plaza in C. P. Díaz, the little town on the other side of the border.[7] Several members of the Eagle Pass Brass Band were friends of ours, and one night one of them, Joseph DeBona, invited my chum, Bell Gillespie, and myself to go with him to the concert. We went and that was where I met Paul Friesen, also a member of the band who lived on the Mexican side. After Joe introduced us, Mr. Friesen and I walked around the plaza a few times between numbers, and he escorted me home that night. I was a very much flattered, flustrated [sic] gal from that time forward. He invited me to go to band practice with him the following night, and all that year of 1896 it was band practice, church, etc., all the time.

Mr. Friesen was 36 years old and I was just 16. He was an old-country German, a very handsome guy with a black moustache. He had just been discharged from the U.S. Army, after fifteen years service. It was a heck of a match for a country kid who had never yet worn a long dress, but my parents thought it was grand because Mr. Friesen had a good position with the Mexican International Railroad, which ran from C. P. Díaz to Durango, Mexico, and continued on to Mazatlan.

Mr. Friesen consulted my parents before he ever said a word to me of his intentions—European style—and the first thing I knew I was to be married. My stepsister had gotten herself a beau and we had a double wedding in the parlor of the Dolch Hotel on December 23rd. Paul and I went on a wedding trip to Durango and Monterey.

From that date on I was no better than a bound slave. There wasn't anything I did or tried to do that was right. My husband wouldn't even let me learn to cook, for fear I'd waste something. He had one meal a day sent from the hotel nearby and that was supposed to feed the two of us. There was nothing too good for him; for me there was nothing at all.

Just before our wedding I found out that my husband was a widower and the father of three living children. After our own baby was born I persuaded him to bring two of his boys home, and the two lads and I became the best of friends. They called me mamma, and respected me, although I was only a couple of years older than the eldest one. The poor kids had spent their lives in an orphanage, their own mother having been dead since they were just babies.

At the end of the Spanish-American War Mr. Friesen treated himself to a trip to New York to see Admiral Dewey come in, and while he was gone the two lads and I put our heads together and decided to do something about our situation. None of us had any clothes, and there wasn't any household linen, except two pairs of sheets mother had given me when I married and a few ragged towels. We had no curtains and very little of anything else. Well, we plumped my baby, Carl, in his buggy one day and headed for town. First we bought a sewing machine, then a couple of bolts of curtain scrim, a bolt of sheeting, another bolt of pillow tubing, a bolt of crash toweling, yards of gingham for blouses for the boys, and yards of dress material for me. After we cut out what we

*Figure 3. Mattie Friesen, taken shortly after her marriage
to Paul Friesen in 1896.
(Photograph courtesy of Marjean Binns.)*

wanted we began sewing. Having been in the orphanage both the boys could make button holes and sew on buttons a lot better than I could.

When that old bird got back home and saw the house—new curtains, new bed linen, new everything—he was delighted for about ten minutes. He said how wonderful it was for Mother Franks to send us all that stuff. But when I spunked up and told him we had made it all ourselves his face turned purple. I think he would have struck me, but I had told him before that if he ever did I would kill him if I had to follow him ten years and shoot him in the back. He screamed, "You couldn't have made it all—you didn't have any money!" Suddenly realizing I wasn't afraid of him any more, I replied, "Oh, I bought it all and charged it to you." I'll never forget that scene—I really thought that man would burst a blood vessel. He swore he wouldn't pay a dime for the stuff, but I told him he knew he would and ten times the amount, rather than have people find out what kind of a tightwad he was.

Things finally got so bad with him picking on the boys, cursing the baby for crying and abusing me for everything under the sun that I left him. He refused to get me a pass home, so I stole money out of his pockets and paid my own fare. It was the boys I hated to leave. They wrote me continually, begging me to come back.

Life wasn't too pleasant at Del Rio, either, with my sister, Bennie, throwing it in my face that after three years of married life I had to come home to be supported.

I began to try to learn something to make a living for myself and my baby. My parents had bought up the old Woods Bank Building, which had been the first bank in Del Rio. They had remodeled it into a nice two-story hotel. "The only first-class hotel in town"—so the ad in the paper read—though it didn't have running water and the toilets were way out in the back yard.

One of the boarders was a telegraph operator named Henry Hall. It was he who suggested that I learn telegraphy. I asked him what telegraphy was; said I'd never heard of it. Patiently he explained, then printed the Morse alphabet for me on a slip of paper, and rigged up a "set" for me to practice on. Well, that slip of paper blew away, so he gave me another. Mother let me put my key on her breadboard and I printed the code beside it. I had two jars of local battery.[8] Mr. Hall showed me how to make the letters and that was all he could do; he belonged to the ORT.[9]

Well, I helped mother with the work and put in every minute I could on my practice. I loved it. When I read the papers or a book or anything I could get my hands on, I'd be sending what I was reading.

It went on that way for about six months, until one day the Superintendent of Telegraph, Mr. A. F. Roome of New Orleans, came to Del Rio and stopped at the Franks Hotel. He was sitting on the front porch talking to my dad when I started sending out of the newspaper; he raised his head, listened a few seconds and asked dad, "Have you a branch of the Western Union here?" Dad answered, "No, that's my damfool daughter, she thinks she will learn to telegraph." (He never wanted me to work.) Mr. Roome replied, "Well, I think so, too," and he came down the hall to where I was, reached over and sent something on my key. I couldn't read it and he wanted to know why. When I told him I'd never heard anyone send, except myself, he told me to go to the depot and learn to receive. I explained that all the operators were union men and that they wouldn't let me practice in the office. He said he would fix it some way, and he did; he arranged for me to sit in the trainmaster's office, two rooms away from the telegraph office, where I could copy anything and everything I heard.[10]

Gosh, I was disgusted and discouraged! For a person who had never heard anyone else send to try to pick out one wire and concentrate on it with nine sets of wires going clickety-click wasn't very heartening. But I stuck to it and learned to do just that. It took me a long, long time but the day finally came when I could copy anything that went over any of those wires—all by hand. I telegraphed for five years before I ever touched a typewriter. The first sentence I completed was when Queen Victoria of England died. The sentence read, "The Queen is dead; long live the King."[11]

I learned to copy figures from hearing the lottery lists being wired from New Orleans to San Francisco and the railroad work and Western Union right there in that room. Then the chief dispatcher suggested I go up to Comstock, a little waystation, to become familiar with the routine away from the terminal.[12] Old Basil Hayden was agent there. I had no money, so to support myself and my little son Carl I waited on tables and washed dishes at the Phillips Hotel (where we lived) when I wasn't practicing at the station.

This went on until one day I got a Western Union message from Daddy Franks to come home at once. I couldn't imagine what was the matter, but since Del Rio was only an hour's ride from Comstock I packed up and went. On arriving, I found that Daddy had a job for me. The U.S. Immigration Service had opened a port of entry downriver and needed an Inspectress of Customs. That was my very first paying job, and there wasn't a prouder human being in all the world. Whether I stayed or not depended upon a civil service examination which would be held in three months' time. Daddy Franks was sure I could pass it—I've often wondered why he thought so, since I had no education. Well, I wore a six-shooter and spent 12 hours a day in a little 6x6 guardhouse along with Bert McDowell, the inspector. We were working under Colonel C. C. Drake, then collector of customs at Eagle Pass. I was supposed to search all females crossing the river from the Mexican to the American side for contraband goods. But all I ever found were six bottles of mescal on one very fat old woman. She had them tied around her waist, which wasn't small after I had taken them off her.

When the time for the civil service examination rolled around I passed it, though how, I'll never know.

This good job was abolished in 1902. I had kept up my practice of telegraphy all this time, but was still a little rusty on the receiving side. I began looking for work and while on a visit to Eagle Pass got a call from the Western Union manager, Mr. Rawlings. He told me he had located a job for me at Sabinas, Mexico, a small place just about 40 miles south of C. P. Díaz. Maybe you think I wasn't tickled! Little Carl and I took the first train to Sabinas. If any Morse operators ever read this, they will know exactly how I felt. When I copied my first train order, it read: *Aug. 22, 1902. No. 2 run ten 10 mins late Diaz to Sabinas*, and it was signed J. F. D., who was J. F. Dickey, Supt.[13] I copied that order without a hitch, but when it came my turn to repeat it, I thought I'd die. My hands seemed to have no bones in them; they wobbled all over the keys. It took me all of ten minutes to calm myself down.

I worked in Sabinas about a month. That good lad, my step-son, Arthur Friesen, was chief clerk to the general roadmaster, the same job his dad, my ex-husband and the father of my own boy, had held in C. P. Díaz.[14] Arthur took care of Carl while I slept days, and slept with him at night while I worked. We had 12-hour shifts then. I got sick but was afraid to admit it or lay off for fear I'd never get another job. I held on until a train crew found me unconscious in the office one night. I never knew how I reached the hotel. After that I took the train for Del Rio and stayed there 90 days, for I had a bad siege of typhoid pneumonia and came very near death.

As soon as I had regained my strength I went back to Mexico, to C. P. Díaz this time, and stayed with an old friend while I tried to locate another job. They were afraid to send me back to Sabinas because the drinking water there was making everyone sick.

It was Carl who got me my second job. We were over at the International Hotel one day and Carl, kid-like, was walking on the top of some bannisters. The chief dispatcher from Torreon was sitting nearby when out of a clear blue sky Carl asked him, "Can't you give my mamma a job? We need some money." The chief—his name was Crip Guire—asked whose kid that was, and on being told that his mother was an operator he got up and hobbled over to the dispatcher's office and asked the force why they hadn't put me to work. When they told him about the typhoid fever and that there wasn't any suitable place for me, Crip told me to pack up and come to Torreon. He said he would fix me up, and he did;

he sent me to Durango to work nights. I asked him if he thought I could hold the job, and he answered, "You can sleep, can't you? We have only one train during the night and hell only knows when it gets to Durango. You get you a little cot, go to bed and lock the door. When that train comes the crew can wake you up and you can OS it and go back to bed."[15]

I did just that. I kept Carl at the depot with me for a long time, but the hotel manager where we boarded told me to leave Carl with them, saying he could sleep in the same room with his son. One night around 1 a.m. I spied a little figure in a nightgown coming to the office. That hotel was fully ten blocks away and the wind was blowing a gale. Soon I recognized Carl and the guard went to meet him, asking, "No tiene Miedo, Hijite?" ("Aren't you afraid?") Carl answered, "On no, escura no come nada." ("Oh, no, the dark doesn't eat anything.") He was four, but I'd taught him not to be afraid.[16]

It was while I was working in Durango in March 1903, that I joined the ORT. When I asked the local chairman for the [application] blanks he informed me that he didn't want any women in his local, but I told him his liking had very little effect on me and to send the blanks, which he did, and I joined Division 28.[17] I'm still wearing my ORT pin—47 years later. That pin, and my union card, enabled me to travel many a mile on the railroads, without paying a cent; and there were times when, without it, I would have gone jobless and hungry.

PART TWO

From the year 1903, when I joined the ORT, I was never very far away from a railroad or long out of a telegrapher's job. Partly because of the prejudice against hiring women there were times when the only "operating" I could do was with a mop or broom; but sooner or later I always found my way back to pounding brass, the work I had practiced so hard to learn at home in Del Rio, Texas, and at the station there.

Somebody bumped me off[18] the job I had in Durango at this time and I was sent to Hornos, a little OS station just beyond Torreon. From there, I went to Paila, then to Barroteran, then to Obayos.

While I was still at Sabinas my stepson Arthur asked me if I'd ever given any thought to divorcing his dad. We had been separated almost four years then. I told him I hadn't thought anything about it, and he said that if I ever did take the notion and needed any witnesses to call on him, as he knew plenty. I told him I wouldn't permit him to testify against his father, and that I had enough grounds, anyway. As it turned out I got my divorce uncontested, and soon afterward married a telegrapher from Nova Scotia.[19] I'd met this operator over the wire in 1903, while working on my first job at Sabinas. He used to send me St. Louis papers and he told me the great things he wanted to do for me and for my little son Carl.

Figure 4.
Mattie Friesen, taken while she was a telegrapher in Mexico, around 1903.
Reprinted, by permission of the publisher, from
Railroad Magazine, *May 1950, 69.*

Out of the frying pan into the fire! From our wedding dinner my husband asked to be excused, saying he had to go up to the office for some instructions. He returned in about two hours, dead drunk. I think I would have made an end to everything that day, if I hadn't had my little boy to think of.

That marriage lasted barely six months, but I was to have another child. This man of mine was forever raving about his aristocratic ancestors, and finally I told him if he was a sample of aristocracy I thanked God I was just a plain Texan. He went into town one day, promising to come back on the local, but I didn't see him for three days. There I was carrying a baby and working day and night in an isolated dump, where there was no one except a Mexican section foreman and his gang.[20] And to make matters worse, Carl had contracted sore eyes from playing with the Mexican children.

The night my husband returned from town I asked the conductor of the train if he had him aboard, and when he hesitated before answering, I said, "If he is drunk please take him on through with you." With that my husband walked in the door of the office. What a sight! He was all puffed up, smelled like a distillery, and lit right into me, snarling that he wasn't drunk and would shoot anyone who said he was. He told me to get the hell out of there and let him run things. Afraid as I was of turning the office over to him in that condition, I was still more afraid of him, so I started into the next car—our office was in one outfit car and we lived in another behind it. I had to climb a ladder to get into it, and just as I closed the heavy end door he fired his gun into it. Well, I almost collapsed, but groping around in the dark, I finally got a few of my clothes together, wrapped Carl in a quilt and carried him to the section foreman's house. I woke the old man and after persuading him to flag the next train, I boarded it and went to Del Rio and stayed there till after the baby was born.[21]

I had to make and sell embroidery to pay the doctor and nurse. Seventy-five dollars I had ready. I never saw the Nova Scotian again, but letters from him followed me around for years. The last one I got was in 1910, when I was in Helena, Mont., with Western

Union. I don't know how he found out my address but he wrote me from Winnemucca, Nev., saying he was several thousand miles away. I just wrote on the bottom of his letter, "Go several thousand more," and returned it to him.

Five weeks after the baby was born I took him and Carl and we went right back to my old job at Obayos and stayed there as long as I worked in Mexico. Then, in 1905, the Western Union opened an uptown office in Del Rio and again good old Daddy wired for me and I came home and applied for the post and got it. This was my first commercial work. The first telegram I sent out was addressed to the Oddfellows' Lodge in Larned, Kansas, advising them of the death of one of their members, and asking instructions for the disposition of the remains.

Now, there is quite a difference between the handling of a commercial and a railroad telegram. The commercial message shows the number of words in the body of the message, in what we call the "check." After calling your relay office, or direct office, you give the receiver the number—each message is numbered—then the number of words in the body, meaning the message without the address, addressee and signature. But at the time I didn't know this about commercial telegrams and sent this one to San Antonio in the same manner I would send a railroad message. The receiver, Jack Nolan, (later editor of the *San Antonio Express*) asked what the check was, got rather sarcastic about hams,[22] and we went to the mat, so to speak, over the wire. Jack and I fought all the time I worked in that office, because I wasn't taking any abuse from anyone. About a year later I went into the office in San Antonio and Jim Marshall, the chief, called to me and said, "Come over here, I want to introduce you to Jack Nolan and I want you two to settle your fight." I told him he didn't need to point Jack out, I could find him unaided, which I did. When asked how I did it, I explained, "This guy looks so conceited and smug!" Needless to say, there was more fighting there and then. But eventually we got to know each other better and seven years later when I worked in the San Antonio office, Jack was one of my very best friends.

At Del Rio I was getting fifty dollars per month and support-
ing two children on it. The Western Union had promised me
more salary if I increased the revenue, but they failed to keep their
word; when they refused to raise my salary, I wired them for relief,
packed up and with the two children went to work for the same
company in El Paso. Del Rio is, or was, on a direct wire to El Paso
and I had been working with the people there all the time. When I
asked them, by wire, if they could use a good operator, they asked
who; and when I told them "myself," they advised me to come
right along. But they were dumbfounded when I arrived there
wearing a dress; they had thought I was a man.

We had no schedules and had to go where we were sent, usually. One thing I never could learn to endure was the smell of a
pipe. One of the operators in El Paso, a big fellow named Pollock,
smoked the rankest-smelling bowl I ever got a whiff of. He
worked a quad[23] table with me and I'd have to run outside and
feed the fish about every 20 minutes. Finally, I gave it up, accepted
a job with a fellow named Schofield who was trying to run a telegraph and telephone business on the same wire, and he sent me
to Oro Grande, N.M. I had to act as a telephone operator for
Almogordo[24] and El Paso, and as telegrapher for Silver City and
some other stations—can't remember them all now. That stunt is
still carried on, but at that time, which was early in 1906, it couldn't
be done successfully. So that job didn't last very long.

Then the Western Union sent for me to go to Dallas because I
was considered a good sender. I had no sooner arrived there than
they sent me to Austin to work during a session of the legislature.
This was in the spring of 1907.

I was pretty tired and worn out by the time I got to Austin,
and as cross as a bear. Try traveling about a thousand miles, sitting
up, with one child asleep in your arms and another with his head
in your lap. When I reported for work the old manager, O. D.
Parker, didn't want to put me on, said he knew nothing about me
being sent, etc. I told him to get in touch with the superintendent
and to stop his talk because I was going home and to bed and he

could finish his wrangling when I got up. When I went back, he informed me that he paid the men sixty-five dollars and the women forty and fifty, but I soon told him this woman didn't work for any such salary. He then said, "You must think you are some operator!" I told him I didn't need to think anything at all about it, I *knew* I was. Then, thinking to frighten me, he sat me down to a duplex, which is a wire used for sending and receiving at the same time.[25] I copied everything that came over with a pencil, and when I finished all the operators were standing around with their mouths wide open—that was a feat none of them had ever tackled. I was hired at sixty-five dollars per month.

From Austin they sent me to Tyler and from there back to Dallas; then because they were short of bookkeepers they sent me to Amarillo for ten days to keep books. When I objected to going to Amarillo on account of having to take the children with me, a woman operator, Eva Boutz, sister to L. W. Quick, who was president of the Order of Railroad Telegraphers at that time, persuaded me to leave the children at the Episcopal Home for Children, not as free wards but as paying boarders. She claimed she would call by each morning, see how they were and wire me daily their condition. She claimed that a doctor would be in constant care of them. I didn't want to leave them, but under the strenuous circumstances I did—and I'll never forgive that woman as long as I live.

Mothers have premonitions, I guess, because one night after I'd been in Amarillo about a week I woke up out of a sound sleep, crying, having dreamed there was something wrong with my baby—he was just past two years old. The dream was so clear and vivid that I went to the office and resigned. The men laughed at me; they said a telegram was hanging on the hook at that moment from Mrs. Boutz, which read, "Just saw the kiddies, both fine."

But I insisted on leaving. When I reached Dallas I called a taxi, and rushing to the home asked immediately about the children and that they be sent to me. After about thirty minutes they sent Carl. When I asked him where the baby was, he replied, "Little brother doesn't act right; he lies on the ground and won't play."

When I demanded they bring him to me I found he was burning up with fever, and did not recognize me and never did again. My baby died about three days later, and is buried in a tiny little grave in the Oaklawn Cemetery, Dallas, Texas. Needless to say a large part of my heart died with him.[26]

I did not shed one single tear for months and months; I felt like I was dead myself. After a long time I went home. I couldn't work, couldn't keep my mind concentrated on anything. I would go to lunch and next thing I knew I'd be back up in the office not knowing whether or not I had eaten.

While I was on leave the Western Union strike of 1907 was called. Of course being a union member, both CTUA and ORT, I wouldn't go back to work for them. I never did and never would scab. I took Carl with me and we went to El Paso, then to Amarillo seeking any kind of a job. We traveled on my union cards, when we could get "squared out." At Amarillo I did a chambermaid stunt for our board and room at a little hotel called The Star. Carl filled the water pitchers and emptied the slops.

At this hotel two of the dispatchers for the FW & DC boarded.[27] One of them saw me in the hall one day; I had my head wrapped in a towel and was sweeping. The dispatcher stopped, stared at me and asked, "Isn't that an ORT pin you have on? What are you doing with it?" I answered, "Well, right at the present I am wearing it!" Then he wanted to know if I was an operator, and if so why I wasn't doing better work than sweeping. I told him that was about the sixth damfool question he had asked me in so many minutes, and replied that I was performing the only work I could procure, that I had to eat and so did my little boy. Then he asked me why I didn't go to the dispatcher's office and ask for work—another crazy question. I told him I'd been calling there daily, and was advised, just as often as I went there, to come back tomorrow. He then told me himself to "come back tomorrow," saying he would guarantee I'd get some kind of job. I did and they sent me to Childress. The evening we left neither Carl nor I had a dime and we had had no supper. But someone had given Carl a hotdog and the poor little kid tried his best to get me to eat it, swearing he wasn't hungry. Well, we compromised by halving it.

We arrived in Childress about 2 a.m., and since we had to wait till 8 a.m. to see the chief dispatcher I sat down in the waiting room and took Carl in my lap, where he slept. Finally an operator came out and not knowing I was of his profession he asked, "Lady, don't you want a room to put that boy to bed? There is a hotel right across the street." I thanked him as bravely as I could, told him I didn't have much use for a hotel, and that I was waiting to see the chief. With that the man said, "If you are an operator you come with me." He took us to the hotel, got us a nice warm room, paid for our breakfast and told the landlady to see that we had everything we wanted or needed—golly, that was the grandest food and bed I ever had.

Next morning we walked out of that hotel feeling like we owned the world with a fence around it, and a gate in the fence. The dispatcher sent me over to Wichita Falls to work days. When I got over there the old scabby agent said, "Yes, you telegraph eight hours, then you sweep the freight house, then you. . ." I said, "Hold it, you are not talking to me!" I walked over to the Rock Island,[28] called up the DS and asked if he could use a first-class telegrapher. He could and did; he sent me to Waurika, Okla. When Carl and I arrived we went to the American Hotel which was run by a former conductor. I told him we had no money but had been sent there to work days. He said we could have anything in the house. I went to the Rock Island and talked to J. T. Bricknell, the agent, who told me they needed another operator but *he* hadn't arrived. When Bricknell found out I was the operator he called the chief, Jim Short, at Fort Worth, and told him a lady, claiming she had been hired by him, was there ready to go to work. Jim said, "Hell, we don't hire women." With that I took the wire and telegraphed him, "Maybe you don't but you sure hired me and here I am." He said he didn't think I was a woman, I didn't telegraph like one, but he put me to work.

That was a real job, a junction. Trains went up the Andarko Branch, main line to Fort Worth and Chickasha. There was a cotton press, a gin and all kinds of things. Our force consisted of agent, cashier, cotton clerk warehouseman and operator—me. The old telephone was always ringing, so some of the boys plugged it up with all the paper and rags it would hold, till somebody wrote up the poor service the railroad office afforded the telephone company, cut the piece out of the paper and mailed it to the superintendent, one M. McKernon, at Fort Worth. He came out and gave us the devil. Then one day a horsefaced, sallow long-toothed, stoopshouldered individual came to the counter and whined "What is the matter with your phone?" I answered that I didn't know. He said he'd been ringing it two hours. I told him he should report it to "that pie-faced editor," who wasn't satisfied with writing us up, but had to report us. Mr. Horseface slunk out of the building and the cotton clerk and agent almost collapsed, telling me it was the editor I had talked to. He didn't come back any more.

Now there was a strike on the Western Union and none of us were handling any of their business.[29] If we heard Dallas calling a station some of us on the line would answer, let them send their business in the air and OK with some fictitious "sine." Our relay contained pen points, paper, tacks, rags and just anything to keep it quiet, though I can truthfully say I didn't apply any of them. I never did molest any of the railroad's property. One night a delegation of some kind, consisting of about 50 men, came to the office and wanted to send a telegram to Washington, D.C. I believe the occasion was when Indian Territory and Oklahoma were declared one and the same state.[30] The tolls on this telegram would have been around $20.00. The night man refused to send it, so some smart guy suggested they call me. Not knowing what was up I dressed and went down to see what was wanted. When I learned, I explained that we were not handling Western Union telegrams and that should we accept their telegram and send it to Dallas— the first relay—Dallas would just put a two cent stamp on it and mail it to Washington. I told the men that this was being done daily, and that it would be much cheaper for them to either take it direct to Dallas or mail it themselves.

They were very nice about it, and wanted to know if a money consideration would change my mind. I told them it wasn't a matter of money but of principle, and that if I was concerned with the money I could go to Dallas and make around $250 a month with all expenses paid. That satisfied most of them, but then up walked a conceited ape, saying "Let me get there. I'll see that she accepts this telegram, or ELSE! I guess you don't know who I am." With that I told him, "No, I don't and that's just half of it—I don't give a damn! I know you can get my $57 job and you are welcome to it. I AM NOT SENDING THAT MESSAGE!" and I didn't. Of course I was called to Fort Worth for investigation and later fired—the only time in my life.[31]

After that crowd broke up, I learned that one of the men in it had remarked, "Who is that woman? By G—, she has spunk and I admire her for sticking to her guns. I'm going to marry her, if she'll have me." One of the force, hearing him, said, "I don't know how the h— you are ever going to get close enough to her to marry her—she won't let a man within twenty feet of that counter."

At Christmas time I got a little box by registered mail from Fort Worth. I was busy on the wire when it came, so I tried to unwrap it with one hand, and not succeeding, decided it wasn't anything of any account and threw it into the waste basket. When it hit bottom, out rolled a little box with some blue cotton in the bottom. On retrieving it I discovered that the box contained a lovely gold and enamel ORT pin with a card reading "Merry Xmas." It was signed, J. W. Kiley. I didn't know J. W. Kiley from Adam, but about a week after that a nice-appearing dark-complexioned gent eased up to the counter, said he had taken the liberty of sending me a little Xmas gift and asked if I had received it. Then he went on to explain about having been in the crowd when I refused to send the Western Union.

He told me a few days later that he had fallen in love with my boy, on getting acquainted with him one day in our outfit car—we lived in an old box which was spurred out near the grain elevator.[32] It was divided into three compartments—kitchen, hall and bedroom—and in the hall there was a big hole in the roof for the pipe of the heating stove, which was conspicuous by its absence. Well, it was raining hard and Carl had shoved the dining table under the hole, put a chair on top of the table and was standing on the chair trying to tie the dishpan to the ceiling to stop the rain from coming in. He was trying to tie it to the wires which had formerly held the stovepipe—there was a terrific crash caused by the downfall of dishpan, boy, chair and table, just as Kiley was passing by. Another time Kiley said he heard someone singing at the top of his voice in the outfit car; he peeked in and saw a mop handle dancing around on the floor, and on the other end of the handle a small boy, scrubbing. That same small boy did all the marketing and cooked all my meals.

John Kiley finally popped the question, asking permission to take care of Carl and me. John was a fine fellow, but he drank, though I never saw him drunk before we married. I told him if I ever did he would have to go. That was one thing I would never stand for again—what with my father and the bluenose from Nova Scotia I'd had all the boozers I ever wanted to see. I told him I loved children, but that I'd die before I'd bring another into the world by a drunken father. He made all kinds of promises which he never kept; anyone who drinks at all will slop over at times. John Kiley was grand to me and to Carl, who adored him. He stayed sober just six weeks—but I must tell about our wedding:

Neither of us had ever seen the other dressed up, when we went over to Dallas to get married. I left on the early morning train, and John took a later one. I went to a beauty parlor, got my not-quite-red hair all dolled up, got a brand new suit and hat and was going to the place we had designated to meet. On crossing the street I met a man who looked familiar and turned around to take another look. When I turned the man had done the same, and did

Figure 5.
Mattie Kiley ("Ma Kiley"), taken around 1910.
(Photograph courtesy of Marjean Binns.)

we laugh! John and I had passed each other without recognition because we were all dressed up.[33]

The first time he forgot his promise I warned him, but he didn't believe I meant it. The second time he had gone to Fort Worth, saying he would be back on a certain day. When he didn't show up I wired him, "It is plain to see you won't be sober and I meant what I said." I never saw John Kiley again.

I was fired, I had no work and no money, so I sold my batch outfit, left my little lad with some friends in Cornish, Okla., and started out to find a job. I could work only about two weeks in a place, until my reference was checked, then off came my head—the good Rock Island had me blacklisted. I worked about a week in El Reno, got the axe; worked a week in Stroud, same thing. I kept heading east, and arriving in Kansas City went to work for the Postal.[34] When I got the axe again I bought a ticket to Leavenworth, Kans.

There was a small depression in 1907–08, jobs were not very plentiful and anyway it was very difficult for a woman to secure a railroad telegrapher's job. I had heard that the Milwaukee,[35] which was under construction in Montana, was hiring operators and sending them to the "front." I called on them and the Western Union and the Postal, but there was nothing doing. The Western Union did give me one day's work, which laid me up for a week. I sent about 14,000 words press from the auditorium where the prohibitionists were holding a conference. The day following that stunt my whole left side felt paralyzed.[36]

I kept asking the Milwaukee for work. They said their wires were down at the front, but they felt sure they could place me and for me to be sure and keep in touch with them. My funds were all gone, in fact I was down to my last seventy-five cents. I figured if I ate supper I'd have to stay in the park all night, so I settled for a cup of coffee and went to the YWCA for a bed. It cost fifty cents, leaving me fifteen. And after I'd had coffee in the morning I had just the ten cents for my carfare to Minneapolis. When I went up to the dispatcher's office, he told me to come back at 2 p.m.

When I had been waiting about two hours—in the Union Depot—a young fellow arrived on a train who had a suitcase and on his lapel an ORT button. Since he belonged to my union we got into a conversation, and I found that he was headed for the front, too. When he went upstairs he was told the same story I had been told. Well, this lad—his name was Mosher—took me over to St. Paul to get my luggage, took me to supper, got me a big lunch, a big box of candy, a bunch of magazines and put me on the train. When I opened the first magazine, out dropped a five-dollar bill! It looked like five thousand to me.

After I'd been hired, I learned that Mosher had told the DS, "If there is only one job, you give it to the lady." Then I broke down and howled. I was hungry, broke, lonesome and just about everything else. I almost got licked because I hadn't asked for aid. I never could bring myself to do that until years later.

P ART   T HREE

I was now 28 years old, the mother of a boy of 11, and, by my
own choice, dependent upon my ability as a telegraph operator
for his support and mine. It had been an uphill fight to win the
approval of officials and fellow brass pounders who had every reason to be critical of a lady op. That scrap was going to continue for
a good many years while I went on working for various railroads,
never staying very long in one place but building up all kinds of
seniority in the female branch of the boomer society. By the time I
hired out to the Southern Pacific in 1916, I had to paste a whole
additional page of references to the application blank they gave me
because it was nowhere near big enough to take care of all the jobs
I'd had during the previous ten years. But that's getting ahead of
my story.

When I reported to Marmath, N.D., on the Milwaukee Road,
in 1908, I was sent to Baker, Mont. At that time the place consisted
of a depot, four rooms, a wool house, livery stable, combination
store and Post Office. Across the tracks was a saloon and a house
of prostitution. That was the first time I'd ever seen women of that
reputation, or a woman drunk. The station was supposed to be
occupied by the agent named Swella and two telegraphers and one
room was reserved for the office. The agent refused to let me have
my assigned room, telling everyone I was a spotter, which forced
me to pay board and rent, while the other two lived free.[37]

Needless to say I didn't take this lying down; I put up a fight. I let the officials know what was going on and told them that if they would come out and make a search they might find out why this man, Swella, was so afraid of a spotter. When Swella found I wasn't going to take his decision about the living quarters, he made some slurring remarks about my character and that is where he let himself in for the trouble of his life. I went to Miles City, swore out a warrant and had him arrested for slander. Again I requested that a search be made. This time it was done and loot amounting to four thousand dollars was found hidden in every conceivable place; under the office, under the wool house and the warehouse. Swella had been stealing from the merchandise cars and selling the stuff to the saloons and honkytonks. At the trial I shook my fist under his nose and told him, "The next time you try to run over a woman you just make sure she is not from Texas!" He went to jail; I don't know for how long.

After that I was sent to a little station called Dodge; it was the first depot west of Marmath. The office was a tiny handcar house, which barely held me and my outfit.[38] My cot fit snug against one wall and the telegraph table, and my clothes in a suitcase went under the cot. I cooked on the heating stove and kept my dishes and utensils in a tub, which was also stowed under the bed. Dodge was listed as an agency, although there never was any agency work performed there, and the mice chewed up the tickets. Once in a while some homesteader would come in and ship a carload of potatoes. I had no tariffs or waybills, so I'd get on the telegraph wire and say, "Somebody tell me the rate of a c/l of spuds and somebody else bill them."[39]

After a time they closed Dodge and I went to work on a work train.[40] My office, the same size as at Dodge, was picked up and placed on a flatcar. I'd board the caboose and away we'd go. The last job on this work train was at Landslide, a place located just across the Yellowstone River from a station on the Northern Pacific called Shirley. This Landslide was just what its name indicated, a mountain that tried its dangedest to slide into the Yellowstone River. Every morning there would be from six to eight inches of gravel and dirt covering the tracks, and the steamshovel and derricks had to move it off before trains could pass. I copied orders for the work train. When the temperature got down around fifty and sixty below and the mountain decided to stay put, they pulled the work train off and I headed south again.

My destination was Oklahoma, where I got my little boy, Carl, from the people he had been staying with. They didn't want to let him go, and had even tried to turn him against me. I took him back to Texas, and we stayed there for several months, mostly vacationing, though later I worked for a while at Houston. This was in 1910.

But I had been in the Northwest too long to be satisfied with the heat of Texas in the summer. That fall I resigned and headed back toward Montana. My mother had decided to keep my little boy with her and send him to school. In Minneapolis I ran across an old friend, and after he left I stayed around a few days, hunting a job. I got one that didn't pay much, but covered my expenses until there was an opening on the Milwaukee, at Minnesota Falls.

This was a little dump about three miles up the hill from Montevideo. A switch engine would hoist strings of cars over the grade, and trains left the terminal light enough to fill at Minnesota Falls and go east.[41] I got hold of some caboose cushions and made a bed of them, located a one-burner coaloil heater and was sleeping in the little dump and boarding at a farm nearby.

This office hadn't been open in years. One night I was awakened by the loudest, vilest cuss words I'd ever heard. I didn't mind the cussing so much as I minded being awakened. I walked to the door, threw it back and saw a man sitting there with a handful of switch lists, a few waybills and a lantern.[42] He was raving because he couldn't find cars to match the numbers on his switch list. I said to him, calmly, "You cut that out!" That man very slowly turned his head—it seemed it went all the way around, like an owl's head—then he tore off down the track, leaving his lantern, bills and switch lists. He ran like the devil was after him; I could hear him scattering cinders as he went and I laughed my head off. Next day he came back, headed west. He said to me, "Woman, do you know you scared me most to death last night! I didn't know there was anyone in this office and when I heard your voice and got my head twisted around, you looked to be fifty feet tall, in that white nightgown." That was Conductor Brown, and if he is alive I bet he will remember this.

Before leaving Minneapolis I had written applications to all the railroads and pretty soon had an offer to go to Grand Forks, N.D. I sent in my 10 days' resignation, and the good chief, O. W. Renshaw, told me, "Kiley, if we can't relieve you, just close that damn office and go ahead." I had to do just that. I relieved a man for 90 days at Grand Forks, and when he returned they sent me to Willmar, Minn. I had mailed a pass for Carl to come and spend his vacation with me, so I waited around and worked extra in the WU at St. Paul until he arrived.[43] I used to pin a shipping tag on his coat, put his pass or ticket in an envelope and send him any place in the United States. When he arrived in St. Paul we headed for Rosebud, Mont. I took the wire examination at Glendive on a switchboard that was fully 15 feet long, without missing a thing.[44]

We went to the hotel for the night, leaving word with the clerk to call us for the train which was due to leave about 4 a.m. The sun shining on my face woke me up and I hustled Carl out of bed. We dressed and hurried down to the hotel office where I lit all over the clerk, bawling him out for letting me miss the train. He rubbed his eyes, looked at the clock and said, "Lady, it's only 3:30 a.m." Holy cats! I'd never seen the sun come up in the middle of the night before. Carl and I went to Rosebud, where I worked a split trick, part day and part night. Carl got himself a job as water boy for some concrete workers.

One day I stuck my head out of the hotel window and called him. He came right upstairs and as he went through the hotel lobby the manager said to him, "You mind pretty well, don't you, boy?" Carl answered, "Yes, I have to." Then the manager asked, "She wouldn't whip you, would she?" Carl said, "Well, she hasn't licked me in three years, but that isn't saying she won't!"

Figure 6.
Ma Kiley and Carl Friesen, Rosebud, Montana, 1910.
The handwritten note on the photo reads: "Nor. Pacific, Aug. 2 - 1910. Left to
right Donnelly - 3d trick, Carl Friesen, "Kiley" 2d (?), Appling, Agent."
(Photograph courtesy of Marjean Binns.)

In September I sent Carl back to Del Rio, so he could go to school, and I went to Miles City and worked for the Western Union. While I was there an awful forest fire swept the area. Ashes fell so thick and fast and there was so much smoke the streetlights had to be kept burning all day. I was told that a Milwaukee passenger train was marooned in a tunnel for several days. My next stop was Helena, Montana—still Western Union. I worked the same table with a woman who was drawing about ten dollars more salary than I, for doing the same job. When I learned that she had scabbed during the strike and was considered a *home guard* I refused to work with her.[45] I wired application to all the roads and was sent to the Oregon Short Line at Pocatello, Idaho, for 90 days.

I arrived there about 7 a.m., went directly to the telegraph office, and when the manager, A.W. Stoker, came to the counter I told him I had come to relieve Operator Fitzsimmons. Stoker's eyes bulged out and he almost swallowed his tongue. "Why, you can't work here," he said, "We don't hire women!" I said to him, "*You* may not, but your superintendent did." Finally he wired B. F. Frobes, the superintendent at Salt Lake, "Your operator showed up with a dress on. What will we do with her?"

The operator who received this message, one C. W. Ott, said it was too good to be delivered by a messenger. Wanting to see the fun, he took the wire to the superintendent himself. According to Ott, the superintendent read it, scratched his head, then slammed his feet down on the floor and howled with laughter. "Well, by G—," he said, "I guess that's one on me—that woman had a string of references as long as my arm and they were all good ones!" Then he wired back to Stoker at Pocatello, "Send her to the company doctor; if he can stand her I guess we can." I didn't know about this till a month afterward.

They put me on the train order wire.[46] Trains run in four directions out of Pocatello, on an average of two trains every five minutes. Word got about that there was a woman in the office and the third trick chief began telling the "lids" (ham operators) that *he* was the lady telegrapher. He used a bug sending machine, making it sound light and quick.[47] He fooled the hams completely and got up quite a flirtation with one hick. The fellow finally called at the office one afternoon and asked me if I was "ready." I asked him "for what?" He was dressed up in his Sunday-go-to-meeting clothes, had a silk hanky stuffed down his collar clear around his neck, and was sweating like all get out. He answered me, "Why, to the show, of course. You promised you'd go, didn't you?" I stared at him a minute and told him, "You may be drunk or just crazy, but I never saw or heard of you before and I surely didn't promise to go out with someone I'd never seen." Then he asked me if I didn't sign myself "su," and I told him that the third wire chief signed himself that way. He didn't wait for any further explanation.

A little later they put me on the Salt Lake wire, and one day Mr. Stoker hemmed and hawed and said he guessed I'd better let one of the boys sit in there this morning because some officials were in town and there would be reports I probably wasn't familiar with. Golly, that burned me up. I said to him, "I've copied the grain report on the Great Northern; I've copied the ink in a number of places; I've copied the news reports in others—what is it you think I can't copy?"[48] He backed off then, just as Salt Lake started in on the ink. I was mad all over, but I made an extra nice copy, with paragraphs, indentations and everything. If I say it myself, it was a beautiful report. Well, in about an hour officials Madsen and Frobes walked in. Mr. Frobes had the report I'd done so nicely for Stoker; he threw it on the counter, pretending to be angry, and demanded, "Who copied this report?" Stoker began to stammer excuses—he had a lady in there who hadn't been with him very long, etc., etc. Mr. Frobes stopped him and said, "Don't bother to make excuses, Stoker, that's the best copy that ever came out of this office." Now did I swell up!

Right after Christmas about four jobs were pulled off at Pocatello, including mine, so we operators got busy and wired everywhere.[49] Nobody wanted us. A few weeks before, however, a salesman for the Union Loan & Building Co., who had sold some stock happened to remark that I was the second lady telegrapher he had ever seen, there being one in his home town, Santa Barbara. When I asked her name, he said it was, Youman. Holy cats, I'd known Libbie Youman back in Texas—she'd worked in San Antonio when I was manager at Del Rio in 1905-6.

Remembering this, I wired Libby asking if she knew of any vacancy for a telegrapher. Her answer was a wire to come to Santa Barbara right away. On the strength of it I requested a pass and made it as far as San Francisco. I went down to the Western Union office there, and got permission to talk over the wire to Libby in Santa Barbara. She told me the job wouldn't be available for two weeks, so I told her, "Nothing doing, I would eat you out of house and home," and with that I turned around in my chair and asked

A. A. Marlatt, traffic chief of the San Francisco Western Union, if he could use a good op. He had been listening to our conversation, and he said he could place me if I'd take off my two union buttons. I told him, "That's easy," unpinned the buttons and dropped them in my purse.

I remember he started me in on the Goshen Junction wire where the business had been hanging for 24 hours.[50] It used to be customary to mark up the time spent in calling a station on the backs of the telegrams that hung, and these were about all filled up. Now when I start after an office he might as well answer, because I never let up until I get him. In less than an hour I had that wire all clear and was leaning back in my chair, with my hands locked at the back of my neck and my elbows sticking out. When Marlatt asked what I was doing, I said, "Nothing." He couldn't believe I had moved all the business.

In May the chief operator, Mr. Converse, came to my table and told me to go over to Sacramento and protest against the eight-hour law for women.[51] I asked him why he picked on me, as I hadn't been in California more than five months and didn't know anyone. He replied, "Because you're not afraid to say what you want to, and that's the kind we need over there." I told him, "Well, as long as that is your opinion I'll start on you—I'm not going!" Fine thing for a female union operator to protest a bill that was intended to benefit the women. Up until then he hadn't known I carried the union cards. I'd been making $150 per month on this job, but losing it didn't scare me any. I just quit Western Union and walked over to the Mills Building and asked the Western Pacific for work.

They sent me to Gerlach on second trick—Gerlach is a division point of the Western Pacific Railroad located about a hundred miles west of Winnemucca, Nevada. I worked there from May until September, when I was stricken with appendicitis and sent to Winnemucca, on a stretcher. A hophead of a doctor, named Hall, gave me about all the physic in Winnemucca and sent me back. In about two weeks I had another attack, and when the WP refused to send me to the hospital I went to Reno, Nevada, on my own. I knew no one there, but one of the WU operators had recommended a Dr. George McKenzie, a fine surgeon. When he met me at the Overland Hotel I explained to him that I didn't have any money, and that the Western Pacific was supposed to take care of me. He put me in his buggy and drove me right out to St. Mary's Hospital. The next day he removed my appendix and a few additional things for good measure.

I went back to Gerlach, but in about two months got sick again and this time mother wired me to come home, if I could possibly make the trip, and that she would meet me in Los Angeles. So I was loaded on the train at Gerlach, and rode the baggage car to Oakland where I was met by good old Jim Fox. I had never seen him before that, but had worked with him a lot over the wires. Mother met me in Los Angeles and we went on to Texas. I stayed at Del Rio about two weeks, then went on to San Antonio for another bad operation.

Mother began coaxing me to stay in Del Rio, after I got up, and thinking sure I was going to die I promised her I would. When my doctor, T. T. Jackson, told me I could sit up for a few hours, I told him, "Heck, I've been sitting up a week; I've even been walking around on the porch outside." He threatened to cut my head off and hide it. He also told me I couldn't do any more work for three years, but I went back to work exactly two weeks later, and kept at it until I retired in 1942.

I soon found that I had done a foolish thing in promising to stay in Texas. When you spend winters in the Northwest your blood thickens up and you can't endure a lot of heat. I have always seen eye to eye with the guy who said that if he owned Texas and Hell, he would rent Texas and live in Hell. I tried to persuade mother to let me break my promise, but she wouldn't agree.

Over the wires I had planned a trip to Canada with two men operators, before they met me and discovered I was a woman. By now their plans had materialized and they kept writing me that if I didn't leave Texas I'd be a dead one. So one day I took my only possession, a diamond ring I had bought in installments, "soaked" it for $100, went to the Southern Pacific station and bought a ticket to Kingsgate, on the Canadian line. I bought the ticket in San Antonio and went right through Del Rio, my home town, at 2 a.m., without stopping. I wired mother, "Am on my way to Canada." I still believe I would have been planted early in 1913 if I hadn't left Texas. When I got up north I felt better immediately, and have never been sick to amount to anything since.

I had wired the CPR[52] at Calgary for a job and got the promise before leaving San Antonio. But when I showed up with a dress on, Calgary officials swore they couldn't place me. Instead they sent me over to Regina. I took an upper berth, first I ever occupied, and what a time I had trying to get my corset on while lying flat on my back. But I did it, and then began ringing the bell for the porter. I wanted to and needed to come down, very much. No porter, so I ducked my head out between the curtains, looked up and down the aisle of the car, and spying a young Englishman yelled at him to bring me the ladder. He said, "I beg pardon?" I told him, "You heard what I said—please bring me the ladder." He did so, placing it beneath my berth and gawking upward. I told him, "Now if you don't want the shock of your life you had better turn around because I am coming down."

At Kingsgate one of the two men I had planned the afore-mentioned trip to Canada with, Jim Whitehead, met me and had me get off the train at Cranbrook, where he was dispatching. He introduced me to all the force, saying I was the best operator in the world—golly, that covered a lot of territory, and of course I wasn't, but in his estimation I might have been. I had met Jim, over the wire, when I first went to Gerlach, Nevada, and also J. D. Henderson, the first of the three of us to cross the border. We had all been working for the Western Pacific; Whitehead at Jungo, Nevada, and Henderson at Dunphy. Via telegraph I had talked to those men for three months before someone let the cat out of the bag and they found out I was a woman. I could have murdered the guy who did it; I was having such a grand time. Jim Whitehead hadn't believed I was a woman until he came and saw me with his own eyes. Later, when I was in the hospital at Reno, he had sent me the biggest box of flowers I'd ever seen—four dozen American Beauty roses, a dozen La France, violets and I don't know what else. It was also Jim who had written me to get out of Texas, or I'd be buried there. The time would come soon when I'd be equally in debt to Henderson, but I had no way of knowing that yet. No one ever had better friends than those two men were to me. They treated me just like I was another man.

For a while I worked for the CPR in Regina, but when the manager ran a man around me in point of salary, because he didn't think I could copy United Press, I got sore and quit. I walked over to the Canadian National, two blocks away, picked up a better paying job, and left that, too, when the Saskatchewan Cooperative Elevator Co., Ltd., offered me $100 per month. I worked a leased wire for that outfit out of Winnipeg, copying the grain markets and wiring prices to all the buyers scattered about at different locations.[53] It was the nicest, easiest job I ever had. Sometimes the whole force would close up shop, go down and charter a train; then we'd be off on a picnic.

Following this, a Mrs. Foster, efficiency agent for the Great West Life Insurance Co. of Winnepeg, talked me into trying to sell insurance. I didn't believe I could do it, but the first day out I made about $75 in commissions, as much as I could earn in a month telegraphing for the railroad.

The insurance company insisted I take a territory, but when I wrote for advice to my friend from Nevada, J. D. Henderson, he immediately wrote back asking me to meet him in Saskatoon because he had a better proposition. He said he was thinking of building a two-story office building in Saskatoon, and he wanted me to act as renting agent for him. But the morning after I arrived there I slipped and fell on the icy street, breaking my wrist. When I finally got down to the railroad depot to meet Henderson, my arm was in a cast, and he sent me right back to Regina. He took it up with the ORT, who paid all my bills till I was well again. There wasn't any more insurance. As soon as my arm healed, I hired out on the Grand Trunk Pacific, to go to the West Coast where they were building into Prince Rupert, B.C. I made the trip but never did report for duty as it was the dangedest looking dump I'd ever seen. It looked like a hole that had been blasted out of a big rock, with wooden steps you had to climb, up and up and up. And there was deep slush everywhere. No sir, I didn't want any job there!

I had come out on a boat from Vancouver, and on reaching Prince Rupert the captain had told me he was going to Alaska to take on a cargo of fish. He said he would be back in a few days, and told me to come down and have dinner with him. Well, I came down all right, bag and baggage, and when the boat arrived I informed the captain I was going to have breakfast, dinner and supper with him until we reached Seattle, and that he might as well dig up something for me to do because I had only twenty dollars and didn't intend paying fare with that. The captain said I could assist the stewardess, and that's how I paid my fare. I had the time of my life on that boat.

PART FOUR

Now I'm getting near the end of my story, which began when I was a barelegged country gal down in Atascosa County, Tex. It's strange how things work out: because a railway telegrapher happened to be boarding at the hotel my mother and stepfather ran in Del Rio, Tex., I got into the game myself and spent the rest of my life—40 years, from my first job to my last—working for the railroads, the Western Union and Postal Telegraph all over the western U.S. and in parts of Canada and Old Mexico.

Writing this story of my life means something more to me than a few extra dollars to pay my insurance and the taxes on my house, though it means that too. But primarily getting it on paper and getting it published represents to me an accomplishment—the capping of my up-and-down, sad-happy, sometimes miserable but always wonderful career as a female telegrapher on the railroads. And it is also one more thing that people told me I could never do, but did; just as I fooled the people who told me I could never learn to telegraph. With this writing business, as with the telegraphy, while there were always one or two who encouraged me, most people tried to do just the opposite. But I always seem to win out in the end, somehow. And, I'm not through yet, though I'll never see 70 again.

To get back to my story, after living in Canada and working for the CPR and CNR,[54] I made my way by steamship from

Prince Rupert, B.C. to Seattle, Wash. From Seattle I went to San Francisco by another boat. I was almost broke by the time I got there and after waiting around for a day or two looking for a job, I telephoned my old friend, Jim Fox, in Oakland. He met me right away and loaned me ten dollars. A few days later I took out my diamond ring again and borrowed a hundred dollars on it. Then I went over to Richmond, got a small apartment and put an ad in the paper for hand laundry, housework and child care. I soon had all the work I could do and made enough to meet my expenses.

But before very long the Bell Telephone Co. sent me to Sacramento to relieve their operator in the Morse department.[55] Lordy, but it was hot in Sacramento, after Canada. I handled commercial telegrams for the telephone company. In two hours I could accomplish what it had taken the other gal all day to do, so the manager, a Mr. Meyer, instructed the chief operator to have me learn recording, so I could work the board when I wasn't busy. I asked the chief operator if she thought I was going to scab on the girls, who were getting the enormous sum of thirty dollars a month, and told her, "Nothing doing. Tell him to take a big jump in the lake—I'm no scab!" But she didn't report this to Meyer and that afternoon when he wanted to know if the head operator had given me his message, I said, "Sure she did, and did she give you my reply?" When he answered that she hadn't, I told him to go jump in the lake. He said the company did not permit their employees to use such language and with that I told him to hire someone else to do his dirty work. I disconnected my bug and started out. He called after me that I could draw my money at the end of the week, whereupon I replied that I would return that very afternoon for my money and that if he was wise he would have it ready—he did!

One reason I got so mad at him—he had asked me if I'd go to Marshfield, Ore., for the Coos and Curry Telephone Co., when I finished with him, and I had told him I would and for him to request a pass. I had waited and waited for the pass, but it never came, and when I sent an inquiry to Marshfield I found that the danged little runt had never let the people know I would go there when relieved. Finally I wrote them that I was available and explained how Mr. Meyer had double-crossed us all. To my surprise, they wired me to come. That was in the summer of 1914 and from there on out I never was without a job. The Coos and Curry Telephone Company's wire ran from Marshfield to Roseburg. I would take the telegrams from Bandon, Myrtle Point, Coquille and all those little inland towns over the telephone and then telegraph them to Roseburg.

While working in this town I received a diamond ring through the mail from a baldheaded boyfriend in Regina—Frank French. We had been corresponding all the time since I had left Canada and he had made me promise to meet him in SF and to see the fair with him.[56] He had written that he was going to send me a birthday present, so each day when the mail was delivered all the gals joined me in looking for the package. When it came it was very tiny, about an inch wide and about two and a half inches long. I was busy on the wire, so I told one of the girls to go ahead and open it and when she did she gave a squeal and showed me a lovely diamond ring. My soul—that package had only a two cent stamp on it! I wrote Mr. French and thanked him and scolded him for his carelessness. He wrote back that he guessed the ring had more brains than he did; he had put it in the mail and told it, "Go find the best girl in the world." And it did, he said.

The town of Marshfield wasn't large enough to support both the Western Union and the Coos and Curry Co. The little outfit soon closed and I went to Austin, Nev., to work for the Nevada Central. I got this job by wiring A. H. May, the superintendent, at San Francisco.

Austin is one of the oldest mining towns in the country. I worked for Jim Hiskey there; his job was Western Union, though it was called railroad. I really had some experience in that place. A *basco* came in one day and filed a telegram.[57] When I asked him if he wanted to send it paid or collect, he said he'd let me know when he found out whether or not it had been delivered. I tried to tell the fool we didn't do business that way, but he began to get sassy and I just walked around the counter, caught that guy by the back of his neck, ran him to the door and flung him clear out in the street. Then I turned on Jim Hiskey and Dan Shea, bawling them out for not assisting me. They protested that I didn't need any help—it was the basco who needed it.

Another experience happened on Decoration Day, or July 4th, or some such holiday. Everybody in town had gone away up Reese River on a picnic, leaving only me and a fellow named Tobin, who was a kind of undertaker. Some time in the afternoon the round-house at Battle Mountain came in on the telephone wanting to know if I would run a special motorcar[58] from Battle Mountain to Austin to bring the body of a Mr. Potts, who had dropped dead a minute or two after stepping off the train. I told Bartoo, the roundhouse foreman, to collect ninety dollars and start the works. After a while I received a Western Union telegram addressed to an undertaker named Kearns, whose place of business was right next to our office. But Kearns had gone on the picnic and I serviced the message as undelivered, giving as the reason the fact of the addressee's being out of town. I was then advised to give the message to another undertaker, and gave it to the little fellow, Tobin. The body got in OK, and about 6 p.m. when people began strag-gling in from the picnic and word spread around about Mr. Potts death, everyone crowded around the telegraph office. After a bit, Mr. Kearns, the regular undertaker to whom the telegram had been first addressed, came into the office and demanded *his* telegram. When I told him there was none for him, he went out and put the matter up to a lawyer, Tony Maestretti, who asserted that I had better deliver the wire to Kearns or there would be trou-ble. I told Kearns to go back to Maestretti and tell him that if he knew as much about law as he thought he did about my business he would make a lot better lawyer than he was at present. By this time, Mr. Hiskey had returned and hearing about the scrap came and asked me what was going on. When I explained, he said, "You are right." Heck, I knew that all the time. What I didn't know was that if that body had not reached its destination within 12 hours without having been embalmed we would have been liable to a heavy fine.

On July 5, 1916 I hired out to the Southern Pacific, Salt Lake Division, relieving another telegrapher on the second trick at Sparks, three miles east of Reno. I hadn't worked a relay job for six years. Being a terminal it was some busy place; it had trains for the Susanville Branch, the Mina Branch, the main line east and west. There were two sets of dispatches and all kinds of reports. But the hustle-bustle didn't bother me a bit; I was very much at home.

In 1917 I brought my son, Carl, from where he had been staying with my mother (my dear Daddy Franks died Sept. 1913 while I was in Canada) in Del Rio, Tex., and got him a job as signal maintainer for the Southern Pacific, at Parran, Nev. The first time Carl heard me cussing a little he said, "Mother, I wish you wouldn't swear—it sounds awful!" I told him to run along and peddle his papers and pay no attention to me. For that matter, I never did like vulgarity or dirty yarns myself. This reminds me of when I was learning to telegraph at Del Rio in 1899 and 1900, where the chief dispatcher was a Mr. S. C. Marks, a big, jolly, bald-headed guy who wore a long beard. He chewed tobacco constantly and every time he took a chew he would offer me the plug. But I had sworn off chewing the day I tried a taste of my daddy's chewin', and he found me later lying under a cotton stalk, deathly ill. So I'd tell Mr. Marks, "I don't want that nasty stuff!" But he'd always reply, "Now you listen, young lady, if you're going to learn to telegraph you have to learn to chew, smoke and cuss!" Much less chew, I never did learn to smoke, either, but I did learn to cuss. After I'd been working five years I saw Mr. Marks in El Paso, and in the course of our conversation, I told him, "I've never learned to chew or smoke, but I can sidetrack any sailor you ever saw!"[59]

All railroaders have to let off steam or blow up. We don't necessarily mean to be profane—the words just slip out. One day Carl's motorcar broke down about eight miles from Parran and he had to push it all the way into Parran against a strong wind. Afterwards he said to me, "Mother, I said all the bad words I ever heard you say, all Grandpa Franks used to say and I invented some of my own." But Carl is a fine lad; he seldom uses any bad language—he isn't tough like his Mom.

Figure 7.
Mattie's son, Carl Friesen,
taken between 1910 and 1915.
(Photograph courtesy of Marjean Binns.)

There were several lovable characters among our dispatchers and telegraphers, and we often had a lot of fun along with our work. One dispatcher, especially, was loved by all train enginemen, agents, telegraphers, in fact by everyone who knew him. His name was A. R. Ludwig—"Armour Refrigerator Line" we used to call him. That man was jolly all the time, and he was witty, along with his numerous other good qualities. One time I had to go to Lovelock to file my income tax report. There wasn't any passenger train available, so Luddy sent a message to a freight train: "Pick up one load at Parran and reduce tonnage to what you can safely handle." The big devil, he was ridiculing my weight. One day in giving the weather report at Lovelock, the operator, Mrs. Stanton, said, "Heavy dust storm from the west." Luddy told her, "Oh, that's no dust storm—Kiley just swept out the office at Parran!" He used to call me "Kiley, my boy," and had all the other telegraphers nicknamed. Starting at Clark, Musa March was "Moosa," next Bill Watson at Fernley was "Little Willie," Jim Lusk at Hazen was "Big Jim," Mrs. Stanton was "Flossie," and lastly the little fellow, Radtke, at Oreans was "Little Runt."[60]

One Christmas we rigged up a phoney Christmas tree and sent it to Luddy. Conductor Shontz, on the local, got hold of a small sprig off a pine tree and at every station some operator added some silly thing. There were typewriter ribbon spools, tobacco cans, boxes of matches and several other odds and ends. When the tree got to Parran I added a little china dog, but I called Luddy on the phone and told him I was sending him a big bulldog. I called the ops all along the line and put them wise to the joke. Luddy nearly had a fit; he got the operator at Hazen on the dispatcher's phone, and told him whatever he did to stop the local and get that dog off, that his wife would divorce him if he brought a dog home. I had already posted the operator on the WU wire—he signed himself "DidLake"—and when Diddy OSed the local he pretended it ran the station. Then Luddy tried to get the operator at Clark to stop the train and get the animal off. When the local pulled into Sparks—Luddy's station—I was on the wire telling him to listen

Figure 8.
Mattie Kiley and husband, William Cropley, mid-1920s.
(Photograph courtesy of Bennie Lou Weaver.)

and he would hear the bulldog's chain rattle. Then Conductor Shontz came into his office and put the Christmas tree on Luddy's train sheet. Luddy peeked behind Shontz, inquiring, "Where is that dog that damn Kiley sent?" Shontz reached into his pocket, got the little china toy and put it on the desk. Mrs. Ludwig told me later that it was one of Luddy's favorite keepsakes.

I was working in Sparks in 1926 when I got in touch with Albert Kuhn again, after 35 years.[61] He was working at Blue Canyon [*sic*] on the Sacramento Division, and I was on the Salt Lake Division. He had heard me on the telephone repeating train orders and OSing trains and thought there was something familiar about my voice. Imagine anyone remembering that after 35 years! So he asked some conductor who I was, saying he'd bet a dollar he knew me. The conductor replied that he didn't know my name, but he had heard that I was from Texas. Albert then began calling me on the telegraph. The first time I answered him, "25-9," meaning, "busy with train orders." Then after a bit I called him back and asked who it was. He answered that he was a friend of my family's and that he had boarded with my mother in 1891. Finally I met him one day on the train, between Blue Cañon and Norden, and we talked our heads off. He discussed my family as though he had seen them the previous week, instead of 35 years before.

I didn't meet him again till 1930, but the result was that we were married on May 2, 1931, the happiest two people in the world. He had been married for 25 years, but his wife, an invalid, had died in 1930. We had everything in the world to make two people happy. We were old enough to reason things out, to have patience, understanding and tolerance and we were crazy about each other. We took an 8,000-mile honeymoon trip by car. We had the brightest outlook and plans for the future: He owned one house and I owned another, and we bought four lots in Reno and erected two more, intending to build our own home later when we should both retire. But on the morning of February 27, 1933, he was stricken with a heart attack caused by having to transfer a whole carload of mail alone, because the Southern Pacific had reduced the force at Colfax; and he died in the Southern Pacific hospital in San Francisco at 1:30 a.m. March 3, 1933. I was at Beowawe when he was stricken and went to him at the earliest possible moment, but there was no hope from the first and I lost the one person I loved best on earth, next to my son.

The next great misfortune of my life happened a few years later. With all the numerous times I've been called on the carpet none was ever for mishandling of train orders—until just before I retired. The railroad retirement plan enabled a man to retire with an annuity sufficient to keep him alive, and many of the old time dispatchers were taking it, necessitating the breaking in of new ones—and what a mess! Some of the new men learned the business in good time, but some of them never learned, and it was one of the latter who caused my mix-up. The station where I was working, Fernley, Nev., was a junction from which trains ran up the Modoc to Susanville, Wendel, Westwood, and on up to Alturas. When a train came to Fernley it had to have an entire new set of orders before it could go out in either direction, to Sparks or to Alturas. It usually took about ten balled up orders to get three good ones from this dispatcher who caused my mix-up, and it was the duty of the telegrapher to call him. Besides copying orders from two sets of dispatchers, selling tickets, filing tariff, making up switch lists, adding up tonnage for trains, making "Cx" reports (cars on hand at 7 a.m.), answering Western Union and other message wires, heading trains into the siding or up the main—then to have to take the responsibility of a dispatcher who balls up two-thirds of the work he puts out is a lot to expect of one. When you work that way for a while you get so you don't know what you're doing.

Anyway, one morning I left an order off my clearance and the train it was for got off without it. One of the very strictest rules was that of listing all the orders on the clearance and repeating this list to the dispatcher, who was supposed to put them in his train order book in the manner you had repeated them to him, giving his OK and the time. This particular train followed some passenger—I've forgotten which—and when it showed up at Patna a train standing there waiting for the superior train saw the signal go red when it entered the block and turned it into the siding, thus preventing a head-on meet. Well, I didn't know anything about the trouble until I went to work at twelve the next night and found the message to report for investigation. The conductor of the train who headed the one without the order into the siding turned the whole story in to the superintendent with the names of all concerned—which was his duty—and luckily for me the trick dispatcher who was just as guilty as I was at home asleep and didn't get a chance to alter his book, which would have made it appear that I was entirely to blame. The good chief, one G. E. Payne, now chief at Sparks, got possession of the book of orders and kept it until the investigation, which prevented any alteration.

They gave me sixty brownies, but they didn't give that dispatcher one single reprimand.[62] In fact, he was promoted later. I kept a copy of one of his orders for quite a while, an order which read, "Extra so-and-so west remain on siding at Fernley and meet so-and-so at Thisbe." When I called him on it he wanted to know what was wrong. I asked him how the h— could a train remain on siding and meet another train miles and miles from the place designated . . ! That is what I had to contend with. I had always been so proud of my service to the railroad, and right at the end of my career this had to happen.

Well, the railroad boys told the superintendent they would not permit me to be discharged, but soon after that a fireman threw his train order hoop and hit me on the head, so I did what the company doctor had wanted me to do for a year or two—retired on disability.

Booming makes a good operator, gives you confidence and ability! But all that service had to be proven before I could get my retirement annuity and was *that* a job! Some of the roads didn't keep records. For instance, the time I worked on the CM & PS[63] was never proven, though I was with them eight months. Service in Canada and Old Mexico didn't count; neither did Western

Union or Postal, of course. It had to be railroad service, performed in the United States. I had changed my name several times and that had to be proven. I had to take a reduced annuity because I was unable to establish that I had put in thirty years working on different railroads. But I am proud of my record, my service was first class, second to none.

All that is already a long time ago. I'm on the shelf now (since 1942) and perhaps having a lot of time on my hands is really what brought me to writing up the story of my life and boomer days. It's so hard to find someone who speaks my language. Anyway, I believe that when a railroader gets too old to work he should be taken out and shot, like they do to old horses. We don't know how to converse with the general public; all we know is railroading.

CONCLUSION

"My Up-and-Down, Sad-Happy, Sometimes Miserable but Always Wonderful Career"

In the first installment of "The Bug and I," Mattie Kuhn, "Ma Kiley," credits Betty MacDonald's 1945 book, *The Egg and I*, with inspiring her to write the story of her life. Though marred by MacDonald's prejudice against Native Americans, *The Egg and I* is a witty and amusing account of the vicissitudes of running a chicken farm near Puget Sound in rural Washington State. The book was enormously popular and inspired the 1948 movie of the same name, starring Fred MacMurray and Claudette Colbert. It is easy to find traces of MacDonald's style—uninhibited, opinionated, sometimes ribald—in Mattie Kuhn's writing.[1]

Although *The Egg and I* had first inspired her to write her life story, it took the encouragement of a professional writer to get her started and acquaint her with the basics of publishing. While living in Napa, California, in the late 1940s, Mattie Kuhn met Con Price, a local writer of western stories. Price suggested that she write the story of her life in her own words. As Kuhn recalled in a local newspaper article about her writing of "The Bug and I," her response to Price was, "Why, I can't write! I only had a fifth-grade education." Price, however, encouraged her to write the story in her own words: "Just put it down the way you tell it. You've got enough natural talent for expression to put the yarn over."[2]

She set to work writing "The Bug and I" using a portable Remington Royal typewriter that she took with her wherever she went. Her granddaughter, Marjean Binns, recalls seeing her typing the first draft of the story on the Royal. As Kuhn stated in the opening section, it was intended to be the story of her partnership with her bug, which had been responsible for what she called her "up-and-down, sad-happy, sometimes miserable but always wonderful career as a female telegrapher on the railroads." She was well aware that she was describing an occupation and a lifestyle that would soon live only in memory, as traditional brass pounders were replaced by machines that never went on strike or departed for higher wages and sunnier climes.[3]

Her original draft was 48,000 words in length, put together in an 11-day typing marathon, written, she recalled, "just the way it came to me." When she had completed it, she read it over and decided that "it didn't sound so bad at that." So she wrote a query letter to the editor of *Railroad Magazine*, asking if he would be interested in the life story of a "hard-boiled woman railroader." As she was no doubt aware, *Railroad Magazine* had begun to publish the life stories of retired railroaders; by the late 1940s, it was clear that the age of the steam locomotive and the depot telegrapher was nearing an end, and many of the articles published by the magazine had begun to take on a nostalgic tinge. She received a cautious response, stating that *Railroad Magazine* had a surplus of reminiscences written by retired railroaders, but they would be interested in reading her manuscript.[4]

She sent them her story, and was surprised and delighted to receive an acceptance letter from them a few weeks later. Although her original manuscript was edited down considerably, she was pleased to find that "the rest is just the way I wrote it."

The first publicity she received as a result of the piece came in April 1950, after publication of the first installment, when her local newspaper, the *Napa Register*, wrote a feature on her work under the heading, "Mattie Kuhn, Local Woman, Begins New Career At 70." The article sketched her life and work, and detailed how she had come to write the autobiographical piece in her retirement years. The newspaper article was accompanied by a photo of her seated at her typewriter, with a picture of Carl and a railroad lantern nearby on the desk.[5]

A letter from Mattie Kuhn appeared in the June 1950 issue of *Railroad Magazine,* after two installments of "The Bug and I" had already been published. She wrote in to tell readers that in spite of a recent automobile accident in which three of her vertebrae were "thrown out of joint," she had taken the bus to Oroville, California, to visit one of the men who had helped her when she was stricken with appendicitis in Gerlach, Nevada, in 1911. Although she did not give his name, she mentioned that he had been a young brakeman at the time, but was now a conductor nearing retirement. Together they rode the California Zephyr, a modern streamlined diesel train, and reminisced about old times. Mattie Kuhn mentioned the young man, Mosier, who had helped her get a job with the Milwaukee Railroad in 1908.[6] The conductor replied that Mosier, now 80 years old, lived in Oroville; together they went to visit him, and talked for more than three hours.[7]

Although it would prove to be her only published work, "The Bug and I" series brought Mattie Kuhn not only a few dollars to help pay the bills, but also a measure of recognition and the satisfaction of mastering a new craft. She wrote a second letter to the magazine, which appeared in the July 1950 issue, to tell the editors how it felt to see her first writing attempt in print:

> If it's at all possible I will try to describe my feelings when the mail carrier delivered the April issue of *Railroad.* A neighbor woman was here and she grabbed the magazine, opened it and yelled at me, "Hey, Ma, here it is, pictures and all!" She then promptly plopped herself down and read it all before I even saw it. How did I feel??? Just about like I did the day I won the civil service examination in Eagle Pass, Tex., in 1901 against three women; one a school teacher, another the wife of the collector of Customs at Del Rio, and the third a graduate of the University of Texas. Me, the green ignoramus: no education,

no schooling to speak of, no experience of life or anything else, but an unlimited nerve and gall. I was dolled up in my mother's black satin skirt and one of her very sheer blouses. Down inside I was scared blue. We didn't know the result of the examination for a month, but I already had a temporary assignment to the job and I was wearing the sixshooter, riding the bicycle to and from work and drawing that enormous check of fifty dollars per month, which looked like a million.

How in blazes can you make up pictures like you do? Just wait until Carl sees how he looked leaving C. P. Diaz in 1899. He was under his own power, walking, but he was a very small guy at that. At first I frowned at the hat. I never wear one now, but after it dawned on me to think back to the styles of those days I realized that the hat very closely resembled my wedding hat, which was made of green chenille, tipped up in the back with nine enormous ostrich plumes pointed to the front. That Mexican hombre offering his wares for sale, I bet that was a package of Mexican *dulces* or *tamales*. It surely is realistic.

I'm so proud of "Buttons and Bows in 1895" (family picture appearing with first installment of "The Bug and I")—it has all my dear family, my favorite being Daddy Franks. I never saw that picture till last May, when it was sent me by the first sweetie I ever had, after we had met again for the first time in 53 years.[8]

I suppose you have noted my attitude toward step-parents is quite different from the usual run. I really loved mine better than I did my own parents. They were better to me and I do believe I made a good stepmother myself.

I'm just stumped for the proper words to thank you for accepting and publishing my attempt at writing.[9]

Even in her retirement, Mattie Kuhn was not content to stay in one place for long and moved restlessly from one city to another in California and Nevada. She was living in Reno, Nevada, when she retired from the Southern Pacific in 1942. In the late 1940s, she moved to Napa, California; while in Napa, she was visited by some of her Texas relatives, including her niece,

Bennie Lou. Later, in the early 1950s, she moved farther south, to Atascadero, California.

She had crocheted for many years, and after her retirement from the railroad, she produced a number of bedspreads, which she gave to friends and relatives. One that she made for her son, Carl, was embroidered with symbols related to his career in banking and his work with the Masonic order. Another, in her words, had "the whole darned history of the Western Pacific Railroad on it."[10]

Although she remained active after her retirement, she suffered from a number of health problems and was periodically hospitalized. At the time of her 1942 application for retirement, she was examined and found to be suffering from deafness, arteriosclerosis, and severe arthritis. Mattie Kuhn was, in the opinion of the examining physician, "permanently and totally disabled," and therefore qualified for retirement on disability. These conditions continued to plague her in her old age. Finally, in the late 1960s, when she was in her eighties, her mental condition deteriorated until she could no longer care for herself. Carl took her home to Reno. She died there on 30 July 1971 at the age of 91; she is buried in the Masonic section of the Mountain View Cemetery in Reno.[11]

Mattie Kuhn left a large and diverse family in various parts of Texas and Nevada, many of whom distinguished themselves in a variety of endeavors. The editor of *Railroad Magazine* commented in 1950 that she had "done a good job with her own offspring," referring to her son Carl; he became vice president of the First National Bank of Nevada and played a leading role in the Masonic order, serving as a 33rd-degree Mason and as a Potentate of Kerak Temple of the Shrine. She herself had remarked in the *Napa Register* interview, "That boy is sure a pride to me. He turned out just the way I wanted him to, and I'm right satisfied with that, because he's the main reason I went to work like I did when I was just a snip of a girl." Carl Friesen died in Reno on 9 September 1987 at the age of 89.[12]

Figure 9.
Photograph taken around 1945
of Ma Kiley and her son, Carl.
(Photograph courtesy of
Bennie Lou Weaver.)

A number of her Texas relatives achieved prominence and recognition as well. Mattie's sister, Bennie, became one of the first registered nurses in the Del Rio, Texas, area. A niece with the same name, Bennie Lou, graduated from Baylor University in Waco, Texas, and became the first certified school guidance counselor in Texas.[13]

Even in death, Mattie Kuhn remains a larger-than-life figure to family members. This was partially due to sheer physical size; according to her granddaughter, Marjean Binns, Mattie Kuhn was about 5'9" in height. Although early pictures show her to have been relatively thin as a young woman, by the time she retired, she wore a size 44 dress. An attractive woman throughout her life, she continued to win suitors even in her retirement years.

However, her influence within the family was due primarily to her commanding personality. Her niece, Bennie Lou, recalls her as being highly intelligent and a "persuasive and domineering" personality who played a central role in family politics. According to her granddaughter Marjean, she had a memory for detail that was "frightening." Marjean recalls her grandmother driving her through a featureless part of the desert near Reno and pointing out the exact location of an automobile breakdown that had occurred years before. Family members also remember some negative personality traits: she had a quick temper on occasion, and had a tendency to act impulsively, traits that she acknowledged in "The Bug and I."[14]

Because of her honesty in telling her story, it is possible to come up with a fairly clear portrait of Mattie Kuhn as a person. It is clear that experiencing the divorce of her parents when she was seven years old, living with her alcoholic, ne'er-do-well father, and being placed in a series of foster homes were traumatizing experiences for the young Mattie, as they would have been for any child. As she said of this period, "My sister and I were both very ornery, disobedient little hellions; we had no real love for anyone and distrusted almost everyone."[15] However, when her mother remarried and she was brought into the large and happy extended Franks family, she idolized her stepfather, Daniel Franks, who she said was "one of the finest men who ever drew the breath of life."[16] Her idealization of her stepfather, contrasted with her negative feelings toward her biological father, clearly created problems in her feelings about men that were manifested in her numerous relationships and marriages. Again and again, she married men who behaved similarly to her biological father and eventually rejected them because they did not measure up to the standard set by Daniel Franks.

This ambivalence about male behavior was particularly evidenced in her feelings about John Kiley. In her own words, "John was a fine fellow, but he drank. . . . That was one thing I would never stand for again—what with my father and the bluenose from Nova Scotia I'd had all the boozers I ever wanted to see."[17] Although she left him when he broke his promise to abstain from drinking, she continued to use his name for many years and in fact even used it to sign "The Bug and I."

Despite all the failed marriages, Mattie Kuhn never gave up her dream of finding a mate who would live up to her ideals and not disappoint her. As time went by, she gradually overcame her ambivalence about men; she learned to be more tolerant of human failings and to accept others as they were. She also learned to avoid relationships with potential abusers. Her dream was fulfilled, albeit for only a short time, in her marriage to Albert Kuhn in 1931: "We were old enough to reason things out, to have patience, understanding, and tolerance, and we were crazy about each other." When he died only a few years later, she would remark, "I lost the one person I loved best on earth, next to my son."[18]

Although her personal relationships with men were problematical, she liked working with men and was capable of having deep friendships with them. For a woman, working as a railroad telegrapher required a complex set of interpersonal skills. She often was the only woman working in the depot; she was seen by her male co-workers as being simultaneously a competitor for jobs and a sexually available female. Mattie Kuhn mastered the art of verbal sparring and banter by which she maintained her status and protected her personal integrity in the depot office. She knew when to be friendly, when to demand equal treatment, and when to tell an obnoxious bore to shove off. She reserved her highest praise for men who treated her as an equal and respected her professionalism. Two of her best friends were Jim Whitehead and J. D. Henderson, with whom she had struck up a friendship in 1913 over the wires and had even planned a trip to Canada before they discovered that she was a woman. Jim Whitehead praised her technical skills, saying that she was the "best operator in the world"; later, when she was ill in the hospital, he sent her flowers. As she said of them in "The Bug and I," "No one ever had better friends than those two men were to me. They treated me just like I was another man."[19]

In her later years, Mattie Kuhn tried to deal with her unresolved grief over the death of her second child, Alva Gedney, age two, who became ill while she was out of town on a temporary assignment and died just days after her return to Dallas. Although she mentions the incident in "The Bug and I," she never gives Alva Gedney's name and incorrectly identifies the cemetery in Dallas where he was buried. While the death of any child is always traumatic, the death of her second boy must have been especially so for Mattie Kuhn; for just as she felt that she had been abandoned by her parents as a child, she must have felt that she had abandoned Alva Gedney in Dallas. Although she went to great lengths to explain her reasons for placing Alva Gedney in a children's home for the few days she was away, it is clear that her grief over his death was unresolved, and that she blamed herself for his death. She wrote, "I did not shed one single tear for months and months; I felt like I was dead myself."[20]

From the 1930s onward, Mattie Kuhn wrote to the Oakland Cemetery frequently, inquiring on the condition of Alva Gedney's "tiny little grave" and requesting photographs of the gravesite. She contacted the cemetery in 1951 after the publication of her article and arranged to have a stone border put in around the small grave.[21]

Figure 10. Tombstone of Alva Gedney Crew, Oakland Cemetery, Dallas, Texas. The stone border put in by Ma Kiley after she wrote "The Bug and I" is visible around the base of the stone. (Photograph by author.)

Recovering Lost History

One of the surprising things about the story of women in telegraphy is how completely it has been forgotten. A quick scan through a copy of the *Telegrapher*, from the 1860s, or *Telegraph Age*, from the early years of the twentieth century, shows that women were visible members of the profession who were recognized for their achievements, at least by the editors and readers of the trade journals. Yet today, few scholars, even in the field of women's work, are aware of women's involvement in this technical field. There are several reasons for this. One is that, as in other fields of women's work, accurate employment records were not kept by the companies that employed women telegraphers, as women were not considered to be serious workers.

Corporate records on the subject are scarce. Most large companies simply did not keep centralized personnel records of their employees during the late nineteenth or early twentieth centuries. This was true of Western Union Telegraph Company and of many railroads as well. Western Union knew how many employees it had at any time, but to find out the names and pay rates of individual employees, one would have to go to each individual office and look at the office ledger book. Few of these ledger books are still in existence.

In fact, of the few records that were generated initially, very few survive today. Many of the railroads destroyed personnel records during the closures that occurred with the cutbacks of the 1960s–1980s.

The companies' lack of recordkeeping was remarked upon by the women telegraphers themselves. Ma Kiley mentioned how difficult it was to obtain a record of her service when she retired in 1942.[22] This was due in part to the fact that women tended to change names when they married, and in part to the fact that some railroads simply didn't keep records on their employees. Many railroads considered women to be temporary employees and therefore did not keep as accurate a set of records as they did for men.

Another reason for the lack of information on telegraphers has to do with the technology itself. Telegraphy was rapidly forgotten as it was replaced by the telephone and other forms of communications; few today understand the critical role that railroad telegraphers played in running the railroads safely and on time.

Recovering Ma Kiley's Story

Although she is candid about the personal details of her life in "The Bug and I," Ma Kiley never reveals her real first name, Mattie. Like many other telegraphers, Mattie Kuhn created a telegraphic persona, "Ma Kiley"; through this guise she was able to express her opinions and speak openly about sensitive subjects in public without actually revealing who she was. Women operators in particular used this technique to allow themselves a public voice without the ensuing loss of personal privacy that would have resulted from using their actual names. Thus, as early as the 1860s, "134" and "Magnetta" and "Aurora" could write letters to the *Telegrapher* in support of women's rights, and even attack men in positions of power, without fear of reprisal or loss of employment. Women telegraphers often used their telegraphic signs to identify themselves in print media; this not only protected their identity from the general public, but identified them to their fellow telegraphers, who could then respond over the line, if they so desired. Mattie Kuhn's use of the name "Ma Kiley" was similar; old-time telegraphers reading her story would recognize the name she had used thirty years before.[23]

However, Ma Kiley's deliberate use of a persona in "The Bug and I" made it difficult to find out exactly who she was. When I first encountered the article, I found her story intriguing; it was the most detailed autobiographical account of a woman's career in telegraphy that I had been able to find. However, I needed to verify the details of the story. I had no way of knowing if the story was factual or just a well-written piece of fiction. As I had discovered previously in researching other female telegraphers, verifying her story required utilizing the techniques of genealogical research.

Researching the lives of women workers from the late nineteenth and early twentieth centuries requires a slightly different approach than researching their male contemporaries'. Men tend to leave traces of their financial and occupational lives; they appear in the census as heads of households, in deed books as owners of land and property, and in corporate records as employees and employers. Women, on the other hand, are likelier to leave records of the milestones in their personal lives: marriages, births, and deaths.[24]

Ma Kiley's precision in identifying names, dates, and places made verification relatively easy. I assumed that she had taken the last name of her last husband, Albert Kuhn; she gave specific details about his death, stating that he had died in the Southern Pacific hospital in San Francisco at 1:30 a.m. on 3 March 1933. Thus I was able to obtain a death record for an Albert Kuhn from the state of California that matched all these dates and places; his occupation was given as "telegraph operator," and his employer was the Southern Pacific Railroad. "Mattie Kuhn" was listed as the surviving spouse.[25]

The details she provided regarding her retirement in 1942 enabled me to write to the Railroad Retirement Board and request a copy of the retirement application for Mattie Kuhn.[26] Her retirement application listed all of her railroad-related service in the United States; in order to verify her claims, the Railroad Retirement Board had obtained statements of employment history from all of her employers in the United States. The most detailed is from the Southern Pacific and lists her salary history from the early 1920s to her retirement. Her retirement board record provides excellent verification of her story, as its listing of her employers and dates of employment matches her accounting precisely.

Her Railroad Retirement Board record also contains affidavits relating to her name changes. In order to qualify for benefits, she had to demonstrate that she had worked at various times under the names of Mattie Crew, Mattie Kiley, Mattie Moss, Mattie Cropley, and Mattie Kuhn. The affidavits testified to her marriages and divorces, and gave dates for each.

The Railroad Retirement Board record contains a date of death certification, indicating that she died in Reno, Nevada, on 30 July 1971. From this date, it was possible to locate an obituary in the local newspaper, the *Nevada State Journal*. This obituary gave names of surviving descendants in the Reno area, whom I was then able to contact. Interviews with surviving relatives confirmed the remaining details of her life story and gave me a deeper perspective on her personality.

The Importance of "The Bug and I"

Mattie Kuhn's "The Bug and I" is a unique and valuable document in many ways. It is the most complete autobiography of a woman telegrapher to have been published and provides a unique, personal viewpoint of a life that was full, not only of struggle and sorrow, but also of excitement and adventure. No other account that I am aware of provides such a detailed record of how women got into telegraphy and what their daily work lives were like.

Although westerns and telegraphic romances portrayed the daily life of women telegraphers, they rarely offered details regarding the actual work, which was usually subordinate to the development of the romance between the central characters in these fictional accounts. Mattie Kuhn's account describes graphically the sort of technically based work that telegraphers—women as well as men—performed; not only was mastery of Morse code and telegraphic equipment required, but also knowledge of railroad rules and operations. One of the indicators of first-class proficiency among telegraphers was an understanding of the subtleties of train orders; Mattie Kuhn's discussion of train orders and their use shows clearly the knowledge required by telegraphers on a day-to-day basis.[27]

The entry of women into technical professions is generally considered to be a mid-twentieth-century phenomenon; however, as the story of women telegraphers shows, the lineage goes much further back. Little research has been done on the lives and work of women telegraphers, though they were numerous in the last century and the early part of this century. Many are still alive today and able to give testimony about their working lives. Yet much of the early history—how women got into telegraphy, how they were viewed by their male co-workers, how they struggled to establish their own identities—is missing. This is partly because the existing history is male-dominated; but it is also due to the unique position occupied by telegraphers in the nineteenth-century workplace. They were "information workers" and "technicians" before these terms existed. Male and female telegraph operators alike were regarded with awe by a public that little understood the workings of the "lightning machine" that sent messages from place to place almost instantaneously. Thus, part of the reason for the lack of documentation of the work of telegraphers, both men and women, is the fact that their contemporaries had little understanding of the work that they did.

Surprising parallels exist between the experiences of women telegraphers of a hundred years ago and the contemporary experiences of women in the field of computer programming. Some of these similarities are technically based; the telegrapher's work, like that of a modern computer programmer, consisted of translating English-language instructions into machine-readable codes. Morse code is, in fact, a direct ancestor of the American National Standard Code for Information Interchange (ASCII) codes used by software programmers. The computer itself is the direct descendant of the telegraph; as Carolyn Marvin observed in *When Old Technologies Were New*, "In a historical sense, the computer is no more than an instantaneous telegraph with a prodigious memory, and all the communications inventions in between have simply been elaborations on the telegraph's original work."[28]

Like women telegraphers, women computer programmers today constitute a significant minority within their profession; 1995 figures show that only 29.5 percent of all computer programmers are women.[29] And despite tremendous gains by women in the work world, another striking parallel exists between women computer programmers and women telegraphers as well: the relative absence of their history in the profession. Ruth Perry and Lisa Greber, writing on women's relationship to computers in the autumn 1990 issue of *Signs*, noted that "research on the history of the computer and its relationship to women still needs to be done because much of the early history is missing. The currently available history underwrites the standard story of the computer's masculine roots. The unwritten history may tell a slightly different tale."[30]

For anyone who has studied the story of women in telegraphy, there is a strong sense of deja vu in these words. They are as applicable to the women telegraphers of one hundred years ago as they are to the women computer specialists of today.

Thus, rediscovering the history of women in telegraphy serves a dual purpose. Not only does it illuminate a little-understood area of nineteenth-century women's work, but it also gives us a deeper historical perspective on the role of women in technology and how women have sought to gain recognition in their fields.

Finally, "The Bug and I" is important as a personal story of struggle and achievement. It is, above all, Mattie Kuhn's story of overcoming hardships and meeting challenges; of sometimes being homeless and hungry, and also of standing up for principles and overcoming discrimination, in order to become a first-class operator. It is the story of her "up-and-down, sad-happy, sometimes miserable but always wonderful career."

GLOSSARY OF TERMS

agent. Railway employee responsible for certain tasks in a railroad station. He or she might be a *station agent,* responsible for all activities in a small rural station; a *ticket agent*, responsible for selling tickets; a *freight agent*, responsible for freight deliveries; or an *express agent*, responsible for handling delivery of goods for an express company.

basco. A foolish or stupid-acting person.

blacklisted. Prohibited from employment due to having one's name appear on a confidential list that was passed among employers.

boomer. A railroad employee with a footloose lifestyle and a tendency to change jobs frequently.

box. Short for boxcar.

brass pounder. Telegrapher.

brownie. A demerit; if a railroad worker received too many brownies, he or she could be fired. Named after George R. Brown, who invented the system in 1885.

bug. A semiautomatic sending key, sometimes referred to as a *Vibroplex.* The bug's lever moved sideways, rather than up and down, as with the original telegraph key invented by Samuel Morse and Alfred Vail in the 1840s. Weighted contacts attached to either side of the lever caused the key to automatically produce a series of dots if the lever was moved in one direction, and a series of dashes if moved in the other. This reduced the strain on an operator's arm when performing fast sending, and prevented *glass arm,* a temporary paralysis caused by long periods of high-speed transmission. The bug came into common use around 1900; the Vibroplex version was patented in 1904. Many operators owned their own bug and took it with them as they moved from job to job.

c/l. Carload.

clear. A wire with no business pending; all messages have been sent.

clearance. The listing of all trains allowed to run on a particular track.

CTUA. Commercial Telegraphers' Union of America; commercial operators' union founded in 1902.

direct office. The destination office to which a telegram is being sent.

division. A section of track under the supervision of a road master; or, a union local of the ORT.

DS. Dispatcher. The dispatcher controls the movement of all trains and must know where each train is at all times.

duplex. A telegraph system in which two messages could be simultaneously sent over the same line; invented by J. P. Stearns in 1872.

flag. To signal a train to make an unscheduled stop.

ground. A wire leading to a metal rod driven into the earth; sometimes buried metal pipes, such as water pipes, were used as a substitute. Operators were required to ground their instruments when a lightning storm approached; failure to do so could result in electrocution.

ham. An inexperienced or amateur telegrapher.

hanging. Transmission of a telegram that is delayed due to the failure of the receiving station to respond.

handcar house. A building for the storage of a *handcar*, a flat truck with four wheels propelled along the railroad track by a two-handled pump.

home guard. An operator who stays with one company; the opposite of a boomer.

hook. A spindle on which (1) telegrams waiting for distribution and delivery are placed, or (2) message forms are placed after being transmitted and before being filed.

ink. Copy made in ink, rather than pencil, on the first pass; no mistakes could be made.

leased wire. A private line used by a company for business purposes.

local battery. The battery providing the electricity used by the telegraph instruments in a local office or way station. Local batteries were typically Daniell cells, which consisted of copper and zinc electrodes immersed in a solution of copper sulphate ("blue vitriol").

motor car. A small, four-wheeled vehicle, propelled along the track by an electric motor or internal combustion engine, used to transport personnel or light freight; sometimes called a *track car*.

on the shelf. Retired or unemployed.

op. Telegrapher.

ORT. Order of Railroad Telegraphers. A labor union for railroad telegraphers founded in 1886.

OS. Order station; a railroad station where train orders are given to train conductors. Or, on schedule; reporting a train passing a station (OSing).

outfit car. A boxcar rebuilt into a bunk car for section hands.

pass. A piece of paper entitling the bearer to free passage on a train; free passes were one of the "perks" given to telegraphers and other railroad employees.

patch. A temporary connection, usually made with a temporary cord on a switchboard.

pull off. To eliminate a job; to move a job to a different location.

pumper. A railroad employee responsible for pumping water into the boilers of steam locomotives; part of the water service department.

quad. Quadruplex; an early multiplexed telegraph system, invented by Thomas Edison in 1874, in which four messages are simultaneously sent over the same line.

relay office. A central telegraph office for receiving messages and retransmitting them to their destinations.

roadmaster. The man in charge of railroad building. A corporate official responsible for building and maintenance in a specified division of a railroad.

run the station. To pass an order station without picking up orders.

scab. A nonunion worker; or, to cross the picket lines to work during a strike.

section foreman. The foreman of a *section gang*. A section gang was a crew of track workers employed to keep a certain section of track in good condition.

semaphore. A system of visual signaling using flags.

signal maintainer. A worker who maintains block signals or semaphore flags.

sine. Sign; an operator's identifying code used over the lines.

spotter. A company spy hired to check on employees.

spur. To place a railroad car on a siding; to make it stationary.

superior train. The train with right-of-way on a track.

switchboard. A panel used for connecting telegraph instruments to telegraph lines that terminated at specific destinations, similar in function to a telephone switchboard. A switchboard typically consisted of a series of brass squares mounted on a wooden board, externally connected to the telegraph lines and instruments, and separated from one another by a short spacing. Connections were made by inserting brass plugs in the spaces, connecting the instruments to the lines. First-class operators had to pass switchboard tests to demonstrate their knowledge of switchboard operation.

switch engine. An engine used to switch cars in a switchyard.

switch list. A listing of cars making up a train.

tariff. A book of rates for shipping goods or produce. Tariffs were often expressed as a percentage of the shipping rate between two major cities, such as Chicago and New York; thus the tariff for a specific shipment from New York to Pittsburgh might be listed as 60 percent of the rate for shipping the same goods from New York to Chicago.

teletype. A fully automated telegraphic sending terminal used for typing messages for transmission to a remote location. The name is simply a combination of "telegraph" and "typewriter," since it enabled an operator to transmit messages by simply typing the message on a typewriter keyboard. In earlier versions of teletypes (the *multiplex*), the teletype would output a punched tape containing the text in Baudot code, the ancestor of the modern computer ASCII code. The punched tape would then be fed into a multiplexing unit for transmission, where it would be merged with the data of as many as eight other messages, and transmitted as a common data stream to a remote location. There, the stream would be demultiplexed and each message fed to an automatic printer, where it would be printed out either on a sheet of paper or on paper tape. Later teletype units transmitted data directly, eliminating the need for the paper tape output. The teletype and its printer are the direct ancestors of modern computer keyboards and printers; designers of early computers simply appropriated teletype devices to serve as input/output devices. Thus, in a sense, computers appropriated the language of the telegraph in order to communicate with humans. Morse operators saw the teletype as a threat since it did not require skilled telegraphers to operate it. Many of the teletype operators were women employed at a lower rate than their male counterparts; widespread use of the teletype beginning around 1915 "feminized" the telegraph industry.

trainmaster. The man responsible for keeping correct schedules, overseeing the departure of trains, and operating the switchyards.

train order. Information on stops, waits, meets, and any other train movements telegraphed by the dispatcher to telegraphers at order stations, who then handed them to train conductors. A *Number 31* train order required the train to stop so that the conductor could sign the order; a *Number 19* train order could be "hooped" to the passing train by means of an order staff.

train order wire. A telegraph line used exclusively for sending train orders to individual order stations.

trick. Work or duty shift.

waybill. A document prepared by the carrier of a shipment containing details about the shipment, the route, and the charges.

wire examination. A test given to first-class telegraphers to verify their ability to set up a circuit using a switchboard.

work train. A train used for railroad construction, often carrying earth-moving equipment, gravel, and rock. Work trains sometimes included *crew cars*, boxcars converted into living quarters, when working in remote areas for long periods of time.

NOTES

INTRODUCTION

Ma Kiley and Her "Bug"

1. Ma Kiley, "The Bug and I," part 4, *Railroad Magazine* July 1950, 68.
2. "The Bug and I," part 4, 98. Note: Page numbering for "The Bug and I" reflects the pagination of this book, not the *Railroad Magazine* serialization.
3. Biographical information is based on Ma Kiley's autobiographical "The Bug and I," parts 1–4, *Railroad Magazine* April–July 1950; *Record of Employee's Prior Service* for Mattie C. Kuhn, Railroad Retirement Board, August 1941; and interviews with her grand-daughter, Marjean Binns, 13 October and 27 December 1995.

"It's So Hard to Find Someone Who Speaks My Language."

4. For a good history of signaling in the early days of railroading, see Thomas Curtis Clarke et. al., *The American Railway: Its Construction, Management, and Appliances* (New York, 1897; reprint New York: Arno Press, 1976); see also Ian R. Bartky, "Running on Time," *Railroad History* 159 (autumn 1988): 18–38.
5. Robert L. Thompson, *Wiring A Continent: The History of the Telegraph Industry in the United States 1832–1866* (Princeton: Princeton University Press, 1947), 206–209.
6. For the language of telegraphers, see Lewis Coe, *The Telegraph: A History of Morse's Invention and Its Predecessors in the United States* (Jefferson, N.C.: McFarland and Co., 1993); see also Minnie Swan Mitchell, "The Lingo of Telegraph Operators," *American Speech* (April 1937): 154–55.

7. William L. Withuhn, ed., *Rails Across America: A History of Railroads in North America* (New York: Smithmark, 1993), 84–86.

8. Robert A. Calvert and Arnoldo De León, *The History of Texas* (Arlington Heights, Ill.: Harlan Davidson, Inc., 1990), 180–81.

9. Ramon Eduardo Ruiz, *Triumphs and Tragedy: A History of the Mexican People* (New York: Norton & Co., 1992), 269, 277.

"I Got into the Game Myself."

10. For a good overview of the types of work women have done for the railroads, see Shirley Burman, "Women and the American Railroad—Documentary Photography," *Journal of the West* (April 1994): 36–41. Burman is also curator of a traveling photographic exhibition, "Women and the American Railroad," which has appeared at many railroad museums across the United States.

11. For more information on Sarah Bagley, see Helena Wright, "Sarah G. Bagley: A Biographical Note," *Labor History* 20 no. 3 (summer 1979): 398–413. Information on Helen Mills is taken from "The First Woman Operator," *Telegraph and Telephone Age*, 1 October 1910, 659–60. Emma Hunter's telegraphic work is described in James D. Reid, *The Telegraph in America: Its Founders, Promoters, and Noted Men* (New York: Derby Brothers, 1879), 170–71.

12. "The Oldest Lady Telegrapher," *Telegraph Age*, 16 September 1897, 382; "Aged Lady's Fall Causes Death," *Lewistown Sentinel*, 24 March 1922, 1.

13. "Mrs. Abbie Vaughan 'Mother of Code Telegraphy' Dies at Home Here," *Long Beach Press*, 19 August 1924.

14. Thompson, *Wiring A Continent*, 426.

15. *Journal of the Telegraph*, 15 January 1869, 42.

16. For a discussion of the employment of women in the post–Civil War telegraph industry, see Melodie Andrews, "'What the Girls Can Do': The Debate over the Employment of Women in the Early American Telegraph Industry," *Essays in Economic and Business History* 8 (1990): 109–20.

17. For a discussion of the strike of 1870, see Vidkunn Ulriksson, *The Telegraphers: Their Craft and Their Unions* (Washington, D.C.: Public Affairs Press, 1953), 23–28. For the attitude of women operators toward Western Union, see *Telegrapher*, 22 January 1870, 173.

18. Ibid., 26 February 1870, 214.
19. *Vinton (Iowa) Eagle*, 2 December 1874, reprinted in *Telegrapher*, 2 January 1875, 1; ibid., 4 September 1875, 213; ibid., 1 July 1876, 159. See also Edwin Gabler, *The American Telegrapher: A Social History 1860–1900* (New Brunswick: Rutgers University Press, 1988), 112, 122.
20. Frances E. Willard, *Occupations for Women* (New York, 1897), 132.

"She Thinks She Will Learn to Telegraph."

21. *The American Railway: Its Construction, Management, and Appliances*, 411; William F. Strobridge, Research Assistant, Wells Fargo Bank, letter to author, 1 December 1992.
22. "The Bug and I," part 3, 76; *The American Railway: Its Construction, Management, and Appliances*, 415.
23. Railroad job descriptions are taken from Ramon F. Adams, *The Language of the Railroader* (Norman: University of Oklahoma Press, 1977).
24. *Telegraph Age*, 1 August 1905, 300.
25. Job and telegram descriptions are taken from Ralph Edward Berry, *The Work of Juniors in the Telegraph Service* (Berkeley: University of California Division of Vocational Education, April 1922).
26. "The Bug and I," part 2, 73.
27. Martha L. Rayne, *What Can A Woman Do? or, Her Position in the Business and Literary World* (Petersburgh, N.Y.: Eagle Publishing Company, 1893), 140–41.
28. "The Bug and I," part 3, 82.
29. Railroad Retirement Board, *Employee's Statement of Compensated Service*, Mattie C. Kuhn, August 1941. Telegraphers' pay rates are discussed in Ulriksson, *The Telegraphers*, 129–69, and Gabler, *The American Telegrapher*, 92–99.
30. "The Bug and I," part 2, 66.

"That Bug and I Really Went Places."

31. Josie Schofield, "Wooing by Wire," *Telegrapher*, 20 November 1875, 277.
32. Rayne, *What Can A Woman Do?*, 139–40.
33. Mitchell, "The Lingo of Telegraph Operators," 154–55.

34. Schofield, "Wooing by Wire," 277.
35. Correspondence, Lynne Belluscio, Le Roy (N.Y.) Historical Society, 14 January 1993.
36. Hattie Huthison's story can be found in the *Charlotte (N.C.) Home and Democrat*, 17 August 1883, and in Ruthe Weingarten, *Texas Women: A Pictorial History from Indians to Astronauts* (Austin: Eakin Press, 1985), 59, where she is identified as a "telephone" operator. Information on Ellen Laughton is taken from Reid, *The Telegraph in America*, 171.
37. For a discussion of education for women in the nineteenth century and its impact on the workforce, see Margery Davies, *Woman's Place Is at the Typewriter* (Philadelphia: Temple University Press, 1982), 57, and table 2, appendix.
38. Gabler, *The American Telegrapher*, 132.
39. *Telegrapher*, 27 March 1865, 70.
40. *Telegrapher*, 27 February 1865, 58; ibid., 1 February 1866, 42.
41. Gabler, *The American Telegrapher*, 119.
42. *Telegrapher Supplement*, 6 November 1865, 13; Thomas C. Jepsen, "Two 'Lightning Slingers' from South Carolina," *South Carolina Historical Magazine*, October 1993, 264–82. The U.S. Census for 1900, which breaks down occupations by ethnicity, shows 58 male and 11 female African-American telegraph and telephone operators—admittedly a small percentage of the 55,852 total operators in the United States.
43. For an analysis of the underrepresentation of working women in the U.S. Census, see Margo Anderson, "The History of Women and the History of Statistics," *Journal of Women's History* 4, no. 1 (spring 1992), 14–36; Archibald M. McIsaac, *The Order of Railroad Telegraphers: A Study in Trade Unionism and Collective Bargaining* (Princeton: Princeton University Press, 1933), 3.

"Word Got About That There was a Woman in the Office."

44. Justin McCarthy, "Along The Wires," *Harper's New Monthly Magazine*, February 1870, 416–21.
45. Barnet Phillips, "The Thorsdale Telegraphs," *Atlantic Monthly*, October 1876, 400–417.
46. Lida A. Churchill, *My Girls* (Boston, 1882); the review appeared in the *Operator*, 14 October 1882, 437.

47. Josie Schofield, "Wooing By Wire," *Telegrapher*, 20 November 1875, 277–78; ibid., 27 November 1875, 283–84.
48. *Telegrapher*, 30 January 1875, 27.
49. Ibid., 15 January 1876, 13.
50. "Marriage By Telegraph," *New York Times*, 11 October 1884.

"Your Operator Showed Up with a Dress On."

51. "The Bug and I," part 2, 61.
52. *Telegrapher*, 31 October 1864, 16; for a fuller discussion of the debate in the *Telegrapher* during the 1860s, see Gabler, *The American Telegrapher*, 133, and Andrews, "What the Girls Can Do." The National Telegraphic Union, or NTU, represented the first attempt by telegraphers to organize a trade union in 1863. Later labor organizations would include the Telegraphers' Protective League in the late 1860s, The Brotherhood of Telegraphers and the Order of Railway Telegraphers in the 1880s, and the Commercial Telegraphers' Union in 1902. See "I Never Did and Never Would Scab" for Ma Kiley's participation in the telegraphers' labor movement.
53. *Telegrapher*, 26 December 1864, 32.
54. Ibid., 27 February 1865, 61.
55. Ibid., 9 January 1875, 9.
56. Ibid., 23 January 1875, 20.
57. Ibid., 27 March 1875, 74.
58. Gabler, *The American Telegrapher*, 131–32.
59. Jacqueline Dowd Hall, "O. Delight Smith's Progressive Era," in *Visible Women: New Essays on American Activism*, edited by Nancy A. Hewitt and Suzanne Lebsock (Champaign: University of Illinois Press, 1993), 171; "The Bug and I," part 3, 76. For a good general view of sexuality in nineteenth-century America, see Janet Farrell Brodie, *Contraception and Abortion in Nineteenth-Century America* (Ithaca, N.Y.: Cornell University Press, 1994).
60. Margaret Dreier Robins to Mary Dreier, 12 September 1907, *The Papers of the Women's Trade Union League and Its Principal Leaders,* ed. Edward T. James (Woodbridge, Conn.: Research Publications, Inc., 1981), microfilm, reel 20. The expression "red light district" may have had its origin in the practice of railroad brakemen leaving their lanterns outside the door at houses of prostitution.

61. "The Dangers of Wired Love," *Electrical World*, 13 February 1886, 68–69. Carolyn Marvin discusses Maggie McCutcheon in *When Old Technologies Were New* (New York: Oxford University Press, 1989), 74. *Wired Love* (New York: W. J. Johnston, 1880), by Ella Cheever Thayer, the story of Nattie Rogers's romance over the wires, was probably the most popular telegraphic romance; the novel continued to be advertised in the telegraphic journals well into the 1890s.

"I Never Did and Never Would Scab."

62. "The Bug and I," part 1, 59.
63. For information about the strike of 1870, see Ulriksson, *The Telegraphers*, 23–28; *Chicago Tribune*, 4 January 1870.
64. Edwin Gabler provides an insightful analysis of the Brotherhood of Telegraphers and the strike of 1883 in *The American Telegrapher*.
65. McIsaac, *The Order of Railroad Telegraphers*, 5–19.
66. Ulriksson, *The Telegraphers*, 67–70.
67. *Chicago Tribune*, 10 August 1907.
68. Elizabeth Beardsley Butler, *Women and the Trades: Pittsburgh 1907–08* (Pittsburgh: University of Pittsburgh Press, 1984), 293–94.
69. Ulriksson, *The Telegraphers*, 71.
70. Ibid., 72–77; *San Francisco Chronicle*, 20–22 June 1907.
71. *CTUA Journal,* August 1907, 810; Ulriksson, *The Telegraphers*, 78; *San Francisco Chronicle*, 8 August 1907.
72. Ulriksson, *The Telegraphers*, 80; *Chicago Tribune*, 9-10 August 1907.
73. *Chicago Tribune*, 10–11 August 1907 and 18 August 1907; *New York Times*, 26 August 1907. For Margaret Dreier Robins's feelings about the strike, see her letter to Mary Dreier of 12 September 1907, *The Papers of the Women's Trade Union League and Its Principal Leaders*, reel 20.
74. *CTUA Journal*, September 1907, 974.
75. Ulriksson, *The Telegraphers*, 83.
76. Butler, *Women and the Trades*, 294; Ulriksson, *The Telegraphers*, 89–91.
77. Philip Foner, *Women and the American Labor Movement: From Colonial Times to the Eve of World War I* (New York: The Free Press, 1979), 477; Correspondence, Lynne Belluscio, LeRoy (N.Y.) Historical Society, 14 January 1993; Hall, "O. Delight Smith's Progressive Era," from *Visible Women*, 171–74.
78. "The Bug and I," part 2, 70.

"THE BUG AND I"

Part I

1. A *bug* is a semiautomatic sending key, sometimes referred to as a *Vibroplex*. The bug's lever moved sideways, rather than up and down, as with Morse and Vail's original key; weighted contacts attached to either side of the level caused the key to automatically produce a series of dots if the lever were moved in one direction, and a series of dashes if moved in the other. This reduced the strain on an operator's arm when performing fast sending, and prevented *glass arm*, a temporary paralysis caused by long periods of high-speed transmission. The bug came into common use around 1900; the Vibroplex version was patented in 1904. Many operators owned their own bug and took it with them as they moved from job to job.

2. A *teletype* is a fully automated telegraphic sending terminal used for typing messages for transmission to a remote location. The name is a combination of "telegraph" and "typewriter," so called because it enabled an operator to transmit messages by typing the text on a typewriter keyboard. Morse operators saw the teletype as a threat since it did not require skilled telegraphers to operate it.

3. A *switchboard* is a panel used for connecting telegraph instruments to telegraph lines that terminated at specific destinations, similar in function to a telephone switchboard. A *ground* is a wire leading to a metal rod driven into the earth; sometimes buried metal pipes, such as water pipes, were used as a substitute. Operators were required to ground their instruments when a lightning storm approached; failure to do so could result in electrocution.

4. The name of the county is generally spelled Atascosa.

5. A derogatory slang term for a peashooter—one of Ma Kiley's rare usages of a racial epithet.

6. *Pumpers* were the men who pumped water into the boilers of steam locomotives. The *agent* (or *station agent*) was responsible for all activities of a small rural station.

7. C. P. Díaz (Ciudad Porfirio Díaz) was the prerevolutionary name of Piedras Negras, Mexico, which is just across the Rio Grande from Eagle Pass, Texas. The city was named after Mexican President Porfirio Díaz, and was renamed Piedras Negras after Díaz was deposed in the 1911 revolution.

8. The *local battery* is the battery that provides the electricity used by the telegraph instruments in a local office or way station. Local batteries were typically *Daniell cells*, which consisted of copper and zinc electrodes immersed in a solution of copper sulphate ("blue vitriol").
9. The Order of Railroad Telegraphers was referred to as the ORT; Mr. Hall was forbidden by union regulations to teach telegraphy to a nonmember.
10. The *trainmaster* is the man responsible for keeping correct schedules, overseeing the departure of trains, and operating the switchyards.
11. Queen Victoria died on 22 January 1901.
12. The *dispatcher* controls the movement of all trains and must know where each train is at all times. A *way station* is a local office, as opposed to the main office located at the terminal where train routes originate.
13. A *train order* contains information on stops, waits, meets, and any other train movements. It is telegraphed by the dispatcher to telegraphers at order stations, who then hand them to train conductors.
14. A *road master* is the man in charge of railroad building, or a corporate official responsible for building and maintenance in a specified division of a railroad.
15. To *OS* a train is to report it on schedule or to report a train passing a station.
16. According to his daughter, Marjean Binns, Carl Friesen spoke Spanish fluently before he learned English, due to his mother's work in Mexico.
17. A *division* is a local unit of the ORT.

Part II

18. To be *bumped off* a job was to lose one's position to someone with more seniority.
19. According to an affidavit attached to her Railroad Retirement Board Record, Mattie Friesen married Alexander John Crew in Eagle Pass, Texas, in 1904. The marriage was also noted in the ORT journal, *The Railroad Telegrapher* (May 1904, p. 611), under "Personal Mention": "At Eagle Pass, Tex., Bro. Alex J. Crew, of Div. 53, to Sister M. C. Friesen, of Div. 28."
20. A *section foreman* was in charge of a *section gang*, which was responsible for the maintenance of a section of track.

21. Her second child, a boy, Alva Gedney Crew, was born on 12 February 1905.
22. A *ham* is a term used by telegraphers for an inexperienced operator.
23. A *quad* (quadruplex) telegraph allows four messages to be sent simultaneously, two in each direction. Thus, there are normally four operators at each end of a quad line, two sending and two receiving.
24. Alamogordo, New Mexico.
25. A *duplex* telegraph allows two messages to be sent simultaneously, one in each direction. Normally there are two operators at each end of a duplex; however, Ma Kiley seems to be suggesting that she was able to send and receive at the same time, a feat that few operators could manage.
26. Alva Gedney Crew died on 23 June 1907 and was buried the next day in Oakland (not Oaklawn) Cemetery in Dallas, Texas.
27. To be *squared out* is to travel free by presenting a union card; the *FW & DC* was the Fort Worth and Denver City Railway.
28. Chicago, Rock Island & Pacific Railway Company.
29. The CTUA strike against Western Union had begun on 9 August 1907.
30. Oklahoma and the Indian Territory were combined to form one state which was admitted to the Union on 16 November 1907.
31. Although Ma Kiley may have been unaware of it, the strike had been officially called off by the CTUA on 9 November, a week before the men presumably wanted to send the news regarding Oklahoma achieving statehood on 16 November.
32. An *outfit car* is a boxcar that has been modified to provide sleeping and living quarters; *box* is slang for *boxcar*. To *spur* a railroad car is to move it to a siding and make it stationary.
33. *Railroad Telegrapher* (March 1908, p. 372) carried the following notice under "Marriages": "At Dallas, Tex., Mr. J. W. Kiley to Sister Mattie C. Crew, of Div. 126."
34. The Postal Telegraph Company.
35. The Chicago, Milwaukee, St. Paul & Pacific Railroad Company.
36. Ma Kiley was suffering from an attack of *glass arm*, or *telegraphers' cramp* caused by spending too much time at the key.

Part III

37. A *spotter* is a company spy hired to check up on employees.
38. A *handcar house* is a building for the storage of a handcar, a flat truck with four wheels propelled along the railroad track by a two-handled pump.

39. A *tariff* is a book of rates for shipping goods or produce; a *waybill* is a document prepared by the carrier of a shipment, containing details about the shipment, the route, and the charges. A *c/l* is a carload.
40. A *work train* is a train used for railroad construction, often carrying earthmoving equipment, gravel, and rock.
41. A *switch engine* is an engine used to switch cars, usually in a switch-yard.
42. A *switch list* is a listing of the cars that make up a train.
43. A pass enabled a railroad passenger to travel for free; they were frequently given to telegraphers and other railroad workers as "perks."
44. A *wire examination* is a test of a telegrapher's ability to correctly set up lines to various locations using a telegraphic switchboard. A telegraphic switchboard is a board covered with brass strips that was used to set up connections by inserting brass pegs between the strips.
45. A *home guard* is a company loyalist with a guaranteed permanent position; the opposite of a *boomer*.
46. A *train order wire* is a telegraph line used exclusively to send and receive train orders.
47. A *third trick chief* is the chief operator on the third *trick*, or shift, usually from around midnight to 6 a.m. Ma Kiley is suggesting that women operators were identifiable by their light, quick sending style, something that the third trick chief's prank seems to disprove.
48. An *ink* is copy that must be made directly in ink, rather than being taken down in pencil and copied in ink later.
49. To be *pulled off* a job is to be laid off.
50. A message or telegram is said to be *hanging* if the sending operator has not been able to get the destination operator to respond, in preparation for sending the message. In some offices, the messages were literally hung on a special hook. Once the operator has gotten the receiving stations to answer and has sent all the hung messages, the line is once again *clear*.
51. Ma Kiley is referring to the laws passed by many individual states in 1910–1913 that limited working hours for women to eight hours per day. The National Consumers' League was instrumental in obtaining passage in many states.
52. The CPR is the Canadian Pacific Railroad.
53. A *leased wire* is a private telegraph line that a telegraph company has leased to a business for its exclusive use.

Part IV

54. The CNR is the Canadian National Railroad.
55. This evidently took place during the merger (1909–13) of AT & T and Western Union, when the combined company provided both telephone and telegraph service.
56. Probably the 1915 Panama-Pacific Exposition held in San Francisco. Ma Kiley makes no further mention of her relationship with Frank French.
57. *Basco* (or bosco) is early twentieth-century slang for a foolish or stupid-acting person. Although she does not mention it in "The Bug and I," Mattie Kiley married William A. Moss in Austin, Nevada, in 1915, and divorced him a year later, reassuming the name "Kiley." *Employee's Statement of Compensated Service*, Railroad Retirement Board, 1942.
58. A *motorcar* is a small, four-wheeled vehicle, propelled along the track by an electric motor or internal combustion engine, used to transport personnel or light freight.
59. To *sidetrack* a train is to force it onto a siding; used metaphorically, it means to beat or surpass someone.
60. "Oreans" is probably Oreana, Nevada.
61. Although she does not mention it in "The Bug and I," Mattie Kiley married William Cropley in 1922 and divorced him in 1926. Interview, Marjean Binns, 24 March 1996.
62. *Brownies* are demerits.
63. *CM & PS* probably refers to the Chicago, Milwaukee, St. Paul and Pacific Railroad.

CONCLUSION

"My Up-and-Down, Sad-Happy, Sometimes Miserable But Always Wonderful Career"

1. Betty MacDonald, *The Egg and I* (Philadelphia: J. B. Lippincott, 1945).
2. "Mattie Kuhn, Local Woman, Begins New Career at 70," *Napa Register,* 8 April 1950.
3. "The Bug and I," part 4, 87.
4. The editor of *Railroad Magazine* in 1950 was Henry B. Comstock.

5. *Napa Register*, 8 April 1950.

6. In "The Bug and I," she spells the name "Mosher."

7. On the Spot, *Railroad Magazine*, June 1950, 125.

8. Her "sweetie" was Edward Sturges. Mattie Kuhn wrote in 1949, "I had not seen or heard of him for 53 years except Jennie [wife of Oscar Franks] spoke of him in 1946. I recognized him on sight and called his name. He had been my very first sweetheart and we were engaged but Mother broke us up. He had the original of this picture and sent it to me May 11, 1949." Correspondence, Bennie Lou Weaver, 10 February 1996.

9. "On the Spot," *Railroad Magazine*, July 1950, 124.

10. Some of her bedspreads were given to the Churchill County Museum in Fallon, Nevada; interview, Marjean Binns, 18 May 1996.

11. "Rating Board Decision Sheet for Mrs. Mattie Collins Kuhn," 4 November 1942, Railroad Retirement Board; interview, Marjean Binns, 24 March 1996; "Mattie C. Kuhn, Once Telegraph Operator, Dies," *Nevada State Journal*, 1 August 1971, 41.

12. "On the Spot," *Railroad Magazine,* July 1950, 125; interview, Marjean Binns, 27 December 1995.

13. Interview, Bennie Lou Weaver, 8 January 1996.

14. Interviews, Bennie Lou Weaver, 8 January 1996; Marjean Binns, 27 December 1995.

15. "The Bug and I," part 1, 49.

16. Ibid.

17. Ibid., part 2, 71.

18. Ibid., part 4, 95–96.

19. Ibid., part 3, 85.

20. Ibid., part 2, 67.

21. Interview, Howard Hooper, Director of Oakland Cemetery, Dallas, Texas, 13 January 1996; interview, Marjean Binns, 18 May 1996.

Recovering Lost History

22. "The Bug and I," part 4, 97–98.

Recovering Ma Kiley's Story

23. As noted earlier, telegraphers' use of signs rather than real names to identify themselves over the wire enhanced their freedom to

communicate with one another on a variety of personal subjects, from chess games to romantic exchanges, similar to modern Internet "chat room" conversations.

24. It is worth noting, however, that women telegraphers are exceptions to this rule in that they are likelier than most women of the late nineteenth and early twentieth centuries to have their names and occupation listed in city directories, to own land, and to belong to trade associations.

25. State of California, Standard Certificate of Death for Albert Kuhn, no. 33-017685, 4 March 1933.

26. Correspondence, Jim Metlicka, Office of Public Affairs, Railroad Retirement Board, 19 July 1995.

The Importance of "The Bug and I"

27. See, for example, Peter Josserand, "Lap Orders," *Railroad Magazine*, September 1942, 89.

28. Carolyn Marvin, *When Old Technologies Were New*, 3.

29. U.S. Bureau of the Census, *Statistical Abstract of the United States: 1996* (Washington, D.C., 1996), 406.

30. Ruth Perry and Lisa Greber, "Women and Computers: An Introduction," *Signs*, autumn 1990, 85–87.

BIBLIOGRAPHY

Adams, Ramon F. *The Language of the Railroader.* Norman: University of Oklahoma Press, 1977.

Anderson, Margo. "The History of Women and the History of Statistics." *Journal of Women's History* 4, no. 1 (spring 1992), 14–36.

Andrews, Melodie. " 'What the Girls Can Do': The Debate Over the Employment of Women in the Early American Telegraph Industry." *Essays in Economic and Business History* 8 (1990), 109–20.

Bartky, Ian R. "Running on Time." *Railroad History* 159 (autumn 1988), 18–38.

Belluscio, Lynne. Correspondence with author, 14 January 1993.

Berry, Ralph Edward. *The Work of Juniors in the Telegraph Service.* Berkeley: University of California Division of Vocational Education, April 1922.

Binns, Marjean Friesen. Interviews by and correspondence with the author, 1995–96.

Brodie, Janet Farrell. *Contraception and Abortion in Nineteenth-Century America.* Ithaca: Cornell University Press, 1994.

Burman, Shirley. "Women and the American Railroad—Documentary Photography." *Journal of the West,* April 1994, 36–41.

Butler, Elizabeth Beardsley. *Women and the Trades: Pittsburgh 1907–08.* Pittsburgh: University of Pittsburgh Press, 1984.

Calvert, Robert A., and Arnoldo De León. *The History of Texas.* Arlington Heights, Ill.: Harlan Davidson, Inc., 1990.

Charlotte (N.C.) Home and Democrat, 17 August 1883.

Chicago Tribune, 4 January 1870, 9–11 August 1907, 18 August 1907.

Churchill, Lida A. *My Girls.* Boston, 1882.

Clarke, Thomas Curtis, et. al. *The American Railway: Its Construction, Management, and Appliances*. New York, 1897; reprint, New York: Arno Press, 1976.

Coe, Lewis. *The Telegraph: A History of Morse's Invention and Its Predecessors in the United States*. Jefferson, N.C.: McFarland and Co., 1993.

Commercial Telegraphers' Union of America Journal, August 1907, September 1907.

"The Dangers of Wired Love." *Electrical World*, 13 February 1886, 68–69.

Davies, Margery. *Woman's Place Is at the Typewriter*. Philadelphia: Temple University Press, 1982.

"The First Woman Operator." *Telegraph and Telephone Age*, 1 October 1910, 659–60.

Fison, Roger. "Is Morse Telegraphy Doomed to Extinction?" *Railroad Man's Magazine*, May 1917, 60–77.

Foner, Philip. *Women and the American Labor Movement: From Colonial Times to the Eve of World War I*. New York: The Free Press, 1979.

Gabler, Edwin. *The American Telegrapher: A Social History 1860–1900*. New Brunswick: Rutgers University Press, 1988.

Hewitt, Nancy A., and Suzanne Lebsock, eds. *Visible Women: New Essays on American Activism*. Champaign: University of Illinois Press, 1993.

Hooper, Howard. Telephone interview with author, 13 January 1996.

James, Edward T., ed. *The Papers of the Women's Trade Union League and Its Principal Leaders*. Woodbridge, Conn.: Research Publications, Inc., 1981. Microfilm.

Jepsen, Thomas C. "Two 'Lightning Slingers' from South Carolina." *South Carolina Historical Magazine,* October 1993, 264–82.

Jepsen, Thomas C. "Women Telegraphers in the Railroad Depot." *Railroad History* 173 (autumn 1995), 142–54.

Jepsen, Thomas C. "Women Telegraph Operators on the Western Frontier." *Journal of the West*, April 1996, 72–80.

Josserand, Peter. "Lap Orders." *Railroad Magazine*, September 1942, 89.

Journal of the Telegraph, 15 January 1869.

Kiley, Ma. "The Bug and I." Parts 1–4. *Railroad Magazine*, April-July 1950.

Lewistown (Pennsylvania) Sentinel, 24 March 1922.

Long Beach (California) Press, 19 August 1924.

MacDonald, Betty. *The Egg and I*. Philadelphia: J. B. Lippincott, 1945.

Marvin, Carolyn. *When Old Technologies Were New: Thinking about Electric Communications in the Late Nineteenth Century*. New York: Oxford University Press, 1989.

McCarthy, Justin. "Along The Wires." *Harper's New Monthly Magazine*, February 1870, 416–21.

McIsaac, Archibald M. *The Order of Railroad Telegraphers: A Study in Trade Unionism and Collective Bargaining*. Princeton: Princeton University Press, 1933.

Mitchell, Minnie Swan. "The Lingo of Telegraph Operators." *American Speech*, April 1937, 154–55.

Napa (California) Register, 8 April 1950.

Nevada State Journal, 1 August 1971.

New York Times, 11 October 1884, 26 August 1907.

"The Oldest Lady Telegrapher." *Telegraph Age*, 16 September 1897, 382.

The Operator, 14 October 1882.

Perry, Ruth, and Lisa Greber. "Women and Computers: An Introduction." *Signs*, autumn 1990, 85–87.

Phillips, Barnet. "The Thorsdale Telegraphs." *Atlantic Monthly*, October 1876, 400–417.

Railroad Magazine, September 1942, June–July 1950.

Railroad Retirement Board, *Record of Employee's Prior Service for Mattie C. Kuhn*, August 1941.

The Railroad Telegrapher, May 1904, March 1908.

Rayne, Martha L. *What Can A Woman Do? or, Her Position in the Business and Literary World*. Petersburgh, N.Y.: Eagle Publishing Company, 1893.

Reid, James D. *The Telegraph in America: Its Founders, Promoters, and Noted Men*. New York: Derby Brothers, 1879.

Ruiz, Ramon Eduardo. *Triumphs and Tragedy: A History of the Mexican People*. New York: Norton & Co., 1992.

San Francisco Chronicle, 20–22 June 1907, 8 August 1907.

Schofield, Josie. "Wooing by Wire." *Telegrapher*, 20 November 1875, 277–78; 27 November 1875, 283–84.

Strobridge, William F. Letter to author, 1 December 1992.

Telegraph Age (*Telegraph and Telephone Age* after 1909), 16 September 1897, 1 August 1905, 1 October 1910.

Thayer, Ella Cheever. *Wired Love*. New York: W. J. Johnston, 1880.

The Telegrapher, 31 October 1864, 28 November 1864, 26 December 1864, 30 January 1865, 27 February 1865, 27 March 1865, 6 November 1865, 1 February 1866, 22 January 1870, 26 February 1870, 2 January 1875, 9 January 1875, 23 January 1875, 30 January 1875, 27 March 1875, 4 September 1875, 20 November 1875, 27 November 1875, 15 January 1876, 1 July 1876, 23 September 1876.

Thompson, Robert L. *Wiring A Continent: The History of the Telegraph Industry in the United States 1832–1866.* Princeton: Princeton University Press, 1947.

Ulriksson, Vidkunn. *The Telegraphers: Their Craft and Their Unions.* Washington, D.C.: Public Affairs Press, 1953.

U.S. Bureau of the Census, *Statistical Abstract of the United States: 1996.* Washington, D.C., 1996.

Vinton (Iowa) Eagle, 2 December 1874.

Weaver, Bennie Lou Franks. Interviews by and correspondence with the author, 1995–96.

Weingarten, Ruthe. *Texas Women: A Pictorial History from Indians to Astronauts.* Austin: Eakin Press, 1985.

Willard, Frances E. *Occupations for Women.* New York, 1897.

Withuhn, William L., ed. *Rails Across America: A History of Railroads in North America.* New York: Smithmark, 1993.

Wright, Helena. "Sarah G. Bagley: A Biographical Note." *Labor History* 20, no. 3 (summer 1979), 398–413.